Dance
is Prayer in Motion

Soul to Sole Choreography for Christian Dance Ministry

Mary Margaret Bawden

Dedication

To Jesus, the real Mover, who has choreographed my heart and transformed me from soul to sole. May all of us who worship the Lord of the Dance follow Him with authentic steps.

Epigraph

"For in Him we live and move and have our being" (Acts 17:28).

Mary M. Bawden

Foreword

For the past 17 years, I have taught dance at California State University, San Bernardino, in technique, choreography, and creative movement. I have also had the opportunity to participate in Mary Bawden's dance ministry, SonLight, and I have trained in the workshops using the Soul to Sole Choreography method. Both experiences have provided me with an opportunity to use my love of physical expression for fellowship within the ministry and throughout the congregation.

At the heart of *Dance Is Prayer-in-Motion* is Mary's love and dedication to God—and her desire to share her passion for dance ministry. She provides clear guidelines that have explicit choreographic intentions based on scriptural foundations. Her practical materials and clear methods bring believers and non-believers to the Word of God through dance; all are easily applicable for churches around the world.

However, Mary brings more than a deep faith into her heart for dance ministry. She is an educator that opens the world of choreographic tools to a wide range of dancers and churches.

Why has it taken so long for a book on church dance to do this? Along with nationally known educator Annie Gilbert (whom Mary endorses in her book), Mary focuses on the basic concepts of dance using time, space, force and body to help dancers use dance skill and the leading of the Holy Spirit to create conceptual dances for worship that include praise, beauty, teaching, celebration, and prayer. The result is dance ministry that works!

Join me in reading this book and using it practically at your church! You won't be disappointed.

"David was dancing before the LORD with all his might" (2 *Samuel 6:14*).

Leslie Bryan BA, MA, Professor of Dance, Cal State University San Bernardino

Preface

I felt God's call into dance ministry when I was 15 years of age soon after I made Christ my personal Lord and Savior. At that time, I didn't know what Christian dance was and I had never seen Christian dance ministry. I just knew that I loved ballet and toe shoes. All of that led me to receive a BA in modern dance from UCRiverside and a Master's Degree in worship years later.

I trusted God's call into dance ministry but released the details for Him to work out. After I married my husband, God led our family to attend Trinity Evangelical Free Church in Redlands, California. During that time, the church staff didn't seem to be interested in dance ministry. Instead, I was content to be involved in Bible study and leadership alongside three children who kept me very busy. To my surprise, the Lord Jesus opened the door to movement when the women's ministry asked me to choreograph some dances for a women's retreat. Only a few months later, pastor Jeff Moore called me into his office and asked me if I would be open to starting a dance ministry at Trinity Church. That was 1994.

Throughout the journey, I searched high and low for written resources and mentors to help me develop a dance ministry that would give glory to God through worship. The task was harder than I thought. There were few church dancers that had a biblical foundation to share. Although some books on church dance existed, none showed me the big picture of dance ministry from biblical roots to the nuts and bolts of practical application.

This book started as a series of notes, which became 10 or more pages and morphed into chapters. All that you read is the result of "help" prayers. God helped me in my ministry. and now, I want to help you the way that God helped me.

Feel free to use as much or as little of this book as you want. In particular, I believe lots of surprises will make your journey into dance ministry much easier. I would particularly suggest that you understand the difference between dance, Christian dance, and prayer-in-motion. In

Chapter 2, take a look at your own motives for leadership and use the leadership test in the appendix for personal awareness. Enjoy the leadership and rehearsal covenant, the eight tools you can access to create God honoring choreography, the four rehearsal essentials, and the six-step process for choreography. Moreover, don't overlook the importance of the genesis method (Chapter 3) because it easily accesses the technical ability of all dance levels, styles and ages (including men). Finally, study the guidelines for costumes, the dance preview, and the breakdown for each rehearsal so that the process of each prayer-in-motion goes smoothly.

Nationally and personally, I want movement to communicate embodied faith to transform hard hearts into soft hearts that love Jesus and others. Dance is prayer-in-motion!

Acknowledgment

During the journey of writing this book, I especially give thanks to Emily Youree, Cheryl Schneider, worship pastors Jeff Moore and Bill Born, my husband Richard Bawden, and all the dancers that have so graciously allowed me to listen to God's voice in many years of reflection and choreography. Through the leading of the Holy Spirit, Soul to Sole Choreography has watered my heart with life changing movements.

May the dance continue.

Mary M. Bawden

Table of Contents

Endorsements

"Prayerfully written, Mary Margaret Bawden provides a wealth of information to bring worship dance into the church. Why should movement/dance be a part of worship, and how can it bring glory to God? Whether you are the pastor of a church, the worship/music director, or a dancer/choreographer, these may be some of the questions you have. Supported with Scripture, Bawden gives basic directions on presenting dance as a sacred and meaningful experience for all."

Stella Shizuka Matsuda, past president of the Sacred Dance Guild, former professional dancer with the Gloria Newman Dance Company, retired professor of dance from Moorpark College in Moorpark California, and director of the Alleluia Dance Theater.

"Mary Margaret Bawden has written a wonderful contribution for all of those engaged in dance ministry. Her theological underpinnings, practical suggestions, experienced insights, and heart for Christ and His Church make this book very powerful. She sees far beyond dance itself, to the hearts that Christ can touch through dance. Pastors (as well as dancers and dance ministry directors) will be delighted."

David Timms, PhD, director, Jessup Online, Associate professor, William Jessup University.

"We who are called to dance before the Lord tend not to be highly verbal. Those with whom we must yoke up for this service are pastors, priests, and music worship leaders, who have behind them centuries of written and spoken dialogue about the use of their ministry gifts. We do not.

"Ms. Bawden's excellent book will help many movement and visual artists better articulate why and how these gifts of expression have an important place in the ministry of the Church. Pastors and worship leaders will be gratified to see that dance ministry is a worthy partner in their calling to edify and uplift the Body of Christ."

Randall Bane, director of the worship ministry, David's House.

"Mary Margaret Bawden's book *Dance is Prayer in Motion: Soul to Soul Choreography for Christian Dance Ministry* is a very practical manual especially suitable for church dance groups. Mary's training and experience over many years has given her the background to create easy to follow steps in creating a dance and planning the rehearsal process with a clear biblical basis for the work. Pastors will find her chapter on the setting expectations and guidelines for dance ministry in the church insightful and helpful."

Mary Jones, founder of International Christian Dance Fellowship (ICDF) and Christian Dance Fellowship USA (CDFUSA)

Introduction

Rhythm Without Soul: Barriers

The black-clad dancer embraced the white material at the front of the church. As her spine curved and her arms cried, I saw repentance. By the end of worship, the Spirit used the movements to break open my heart.

As a communication tool in the 21st century, dance ministry "speaks" from soul to sole in a universal language. Research shows that only seven percent of communication includes the spoken word by itself.[1] According to "Nonverbal Communication Theories," wordless cues include body language, tone, and appearance in much greater significance than we recognize.[2] That's what makes dance so powerful. As the gospel is shared visually, intentional choreography transforms, communicates, and convicts people to function according to His design. That knowledge forges our call into dance ministry.

But Jesus beckons us with another call. It concerns more than dance presentation. Secular dance institutions distort the intended purpose for dance while historical church aversion ignores it. Confusion exists. As supporters of dance education, we must change this. The information style of the 21st century requires innovation in ministry communication. The road map to the current technological generation demands visual, creative, personal, and experiential styles. Dance fits this definition perfectly. However, the church may not "get it" yet.

---

[1] A. Mehrabian. (1981) *Silent messages: Implicit communication of emotions and attitudes.* Belmont, CA: Wadsworth, (currently being distributed by Albert Mehrabian, am@kaaj.com.

[2] Republished with permission of Sage Publications, Inc. Books from *Encyclopedia of Communication Theory*, "Nonverbal Communication Theories," Stephen W. Littlejohn and Karen A. Foss, 2009); permission conveyed through Copyright Clearance Center, Inc.

When concise education tools, biblical clarity, and practical, targeted intent form the foundation for presented choreography, the universal, non-verbal language of dance communicates worship movement from soul to sole. On the other hand, when we don't navigate dance ministry with knowledge and skill, or work with inadequate resources, sometimes barricades appear that prevent movement from achieving transcendent purpose.

A negative exposure to dance often shuts the door to future acceptance. Some in Christendom fear body movement but the intimacy of the body should not disqualify dance as a form of communication. In fact, the intimacy of dance naturally projects complex ideas through seemingly simple, pure movement.

We twist inside when we hear worried comments about the art form we love. Of course, THEY can reflect the problem; on the other hand, we need to remedy ministry confusion regarding the use of dance as much as we can. The balance of truth involves ownership. If we own our own issues and resolve them internally, we can eliminate the resistance to dance on our side of the stage. The rest of the resolution belongs to Jesus.

Can you identify with any of these barriers?

Barrier One: I didn't even know that I was asleep until I heard the phone reverberating. It was 5:30 a.m. I yanked my pillow to the side as two fingers groped for the phone handle. The cheery voice said, "Are you the Soul to Sole Mary Bawden?" I sighed affirmation. My husband rolled over and groaned.

"Well, I'm calling from New Joysey. My church is starting a dance team, and we can't find any practical materials to help us. Where can we get some?"

Solution: Nationally, we need Christian dance resources to support the ministries that are exploding everywhere.

Barrier Two: The Christian dance concert began. I sat in my seat and strained to hear the song. The ladies came onto the stage teetering in toe shoes with costumes that showed skin falling forward. I looked away, and then I looked again. The group smiled as they moved; I knew they were trying to say something, but I didn't get it. Ministry? A woman next to me shoved my elbow and said, "Those swans would make a big splash, wouldn't they?" The snickers around me shut out the silence. I knew my ears were turning red; actually, they were hot. Then I shoved the worship folder to the floor and moved in my seat. Finally, it was over.

Solution: We need to define what Christian dance ministry is and use that definition to develop clear ministry guidelines with targeted choreographic intent.

Barrier Three: The trained dancer asked me to come to coffee and pray about ministry. Jen was surprised to hear the new pastor wanted to meet with her personally. His earlier comment dried her heart: "I have never seen dance used effectively for ministry communication." Fear seeped through her skin and stole her peace.

Solution: We need to educate pastors about the relevance of dance ministry with articulate goals.

Barrier Four: God anointed Machelle to dance radiantly and faithfully. She knew it, and I saw it. We talked the morning after the meeting with the church programming committee. They desired "trained dancers" for the Easter service—"real" dancers. The church yearned to develop a dance ministry with professionals that would choreograph soul to sole movement and transform lives.

Solution: We need to validate the relevance of trained and untrained dancers, and provide movement tools that access all technical levels.

Barrier Five: I knew that dance was supposed to touch my soul and give me hope, but it didn't. They danced with skill and training. Technically, it was the best group I had ever seen. But the movement had nothing to do with the message of the song. The applause came from the appreciation of dance skill, not dance ministry. I walked out of church feeling sad.

Solution: We need to make sure technical dance skill never ranks above a relevant gospel message.

Barrier Six: I was embarrassed by what I saw. And I knew the seekers sitting next to me thought the dance was funny. Because it was. The skinny woman in the bright green dress wore a costume that was a size too small. Fortunately, she didn't have a bust that choreographed its own song. But if she had, that movement would have been more interesting than the dance on stage. Confidently, she placed herself in the front for the audience. At the same time, the children in the back missed the meter entirely. The ribbons tangled together, and in the middle of the dance, their colors moved back and forth like half-chewed taffy. On the other side of the stage, two men wearing blousey shirts with visible edges carried flags as they hopped; I never saw their faces. With a dip, they completed the movement in a chorus that repeated over and over and over again. Unfortunately, the chosen song had no theological content. The final section of the choreography ended with a turning crystal ball and a smoke machine that had no relevance to anything.

Solution: We need to set up accountability structures inside dance ministry so that we do not present dances that do not reflect a gospel message in costuming, choreography or worship.

Barrier Seven: But pastor, the dancer only touched her thigh because of a weight exchange. It kept her safe. Why do I have to cut that part of the dance?

Solution: We need to be submissive to church leadership and have a sweet spirit, even though we don't always agree with leadership decisions.

For those of us who live with a passion for dance ministry, there is much to do. But the goal is transcendent. We need to understand what Christian dance ministry is and craft choreography that targets biblical messages. A clear, scriptural foundation will set the stage for Soul to Sole Choreography. Just as critical, we must not avoid the issues that cause internal tension. We must face them with courage so that we can stand in unity before a church that looks sideways at our gifts.

Chapter One

Soul to Sole Foundation

You are the healing
the loving
the touching

You are the laughing
You are the dancing

Jesus, Verb of God
You are the moving—move in me.

-Author unknown

I want to be a verb like Jesus—a verb follower.
I want the life of Jesus to move in me.
Jesus showed me that real movements come from His life—the inside and outside, from soul to sole. And I thought: Do my movements do that?

When I studied dance formally, I wondered: Does the art of dance do that? And later I looked deeper into faith and asked myself: Does Christian dance do that? Does it reflect my faith?

Throughout the years, I've watched many people dance for Jesus—trained dancers, untrained dancers, young people, old people, and children. Sometimes I've seen Jesus transform my heart as I've watched. But sometimes I've ached and stumbled away at lost opportunities because the movement didn't translate. And those failed dances caused me to ask hard questions: Do I put His life in my daily actions? When I share my faith through dance ministry, do I choreograph "living water" (the gospel) into the hearts of those who watch?

> *"Jesus answered her, 'If you knew the gift of God and who it is that asks you for a drink, you would have asked him and he would have given you living water.' 'Sir,' the woman said, 'you have nothing to draw with and the well is deep. Where can you get this living water? Are you greater than our father Jacob, who gave us the well and drank from it himself, as did also his sons and his livestock?'" (John 4:10-12)*[3]

When does a dance become "living water"? What makes it reflect Jesus? And how do we evaluate its success? If we, who love dance, don't know how to answer these questions, the lack of knowledge will produce lives and dances that lack power and clarity. The Bible teaches us this principle is true: "My people are destroyed from lack of knowledge," (Hosea 4:6). Good intentions do not necessarily translate into embodied faith.

---

[3] All Scripture quotations, unless otherwise indicated, are taken from the Holy Bible, New International Version®, NIV®. Copyright ©1973, 1978, 1984, 2011 by Biblica, Inc® Used by permission of Zondervan. All rights reserved worldwide. www.zondervan.com. The "NIV" and "New International Version" are trademarks registered in the United States Patent and Trademark Office by Biblica, Inc.™

GLORIFYING GOD WITH BODY TALK

God, the Master Choreographer, is a mover. And so are His people. In Genesis 1:2, God initiated the dance and soloed as its first dancer. His Spirit "was hovering over the waters." In Acts 17:28, He revealed that "for in him we live and move and have our being." We have our being and our bodies in Him—living water.

In the Old Testament, Scripture says the body God designed for His creatures is good (Genesis 1:31). In the New Testament, this good body becomes the Temple of the Holy Spirit: "Do you not know that your bodies are temples of the Holy Spirit, who is in you, whom you have received from God?" (1 Corinthians 6:19). That means the goal of dancing believers is to glorify Christ by embodying movement that transforms. Second Corinthians 3:18 says, "And we all, who with unveiled faces contemplate the Lord's glory, are being transformed into his image with ever-increasing glory, which comes from the Lord, who is the Spirit."

The use of the body, in a profound way, is pivotal to the message of the gospel of Jesus Christ. God formed humans out of the dust to create a physical body. God sent His Son Jesus, as the Word-in-Flesh, to be incarnated in a body. God gave all believers in the New Testament the gift of the indwelt Spirit inside the temple of the body. In Scripture, heaven is described as a place that will be filled with believers having resurrection bodies. Finally, God designed the body as an intentional holy vehicle for the worship of Him: "Therefore, I urge you, brothers and sisters, in view of God's mercy, to offer your bodies as a living sacrifice, holy and pleasing to God—this is your true and proper worship" (Romans 12:1). In God's eyes, a body giving glory to Him is a powerful, purposeful instrument.

But there's more. God's chosen vehicle for worship has another major function. The body speaks in a universal language. Everyone has a body and everyone uses that body to communicate with others. In M. Adams' article "Every Move You Make," the author states, "Non-verbal communication is our first language. Babies make themselves understood without words."[4]

God formed the body to talk using movement patterns that words stumble to access. Jesus spoke with His actions just as much as He spoke with His words.

"Hence it is appropriate that we use movement to enrich our personal knowledge of Christ whom we approach by faith with our whole selves, not only our intellect" said Sara Savage in the written piece "Through Dance, Fully Human."[5] Of course, this awareness does not discount the usefulness and the power of the spoken/written word. It simply identifies a fact about non-verbal communication that we often fail to acknowledge.

World famous UCLA psychologist Albert Mehrabian researched non-verbal communication (i.e., communication that is not spoken or written) and discovered some startling statistics. He found that only 7 percent of what is understood comes through the spoken word. Fully 55 percent of what people understand comes from non-verbal facial expression with 38 percent resulting from the tone of voice.[6]

Other research reveals even more. "Nonverbal signals can be used without verbal communication to convey messages; when nonverbal behavior does not effectively communicate a message, verbal methods are used to enhance understanding."[7]

Therefore, with God crafting the blueprint for human beings, it is not surprising to learn that non-verbal movement has the potential to paint biblical truth using a sensory language that everyone can understand.

Webster's Dictionary defines sensory as: the faculty of perceiving by means of sight, hearing, smell, taste, or touch.

---

[4]   M. Adams, "Every Move You Make," *Successful Meetings*, 1996, 45-46.

[5]   Sara Savage, "Through Dance, Fully Human," in Beholding the Glory: Incarnation Through the Arts, ed. Jeremy Begbie (Grand Rapids, MI: Baker Academics, 2000), 66. Fair use.

[6] A. Mehrabian. (1981.) *Silent messages: Implicit communication of emotions and attitudes.* Belmont, CA: Wadsworth, (currently being distributed by Albert Mehrabian, am@kaaj.com.

[7] Republished with permission of Thomas Learning, *Nonverbal Communication in Human Interaction*, Mark L. Knapp and Judith A. Hall, 5th edition, 2007; permission conveyed through Copyright Clearance Center, Inc.

In his book introduction, Jeremy Begbie said, "Our concern then is what we might call 'theology through the arts.' This means giving the arts space to do their own work as they engage with the primary testimony of Scripture and with the wealth of Christian traditions. It means that unfamiliar theological themes are uncovered, familiar topics exposed and negotiated in fresh and telling ways, obscure matters clarified, and distortions of truth avoided and even corrected . . . . It also means benefitting from the extraordinary integrative powers of the arts, their ability to reunite the intellect with the other facets of our human make-up—our bodies, wills, emotional life, and so on."[8]

I agree with Jeremy Begbie. In the church, we need to value the arts and use their sensory design to reach a broken world. Jesus Himself modeled the transformative power of the arts with an endless array of words and movements used to show us truth (Matthew 7:24; John 4:13; 6:51;12:36). In the Bible, we find ourselves welcomed into creative stories and parables molded with images and symbols that stir our imaginations. God's personal love story is filled with bread that is packaged in heaven, a rock that helps us persevere, water that lives, and light that we can trust. These examples flood Scripture over and over again with authority because Abba Father delights to show us faith that travels on sensory pathways. Let's use them to let everyone see the Lord of the Dance as Scripture reveals Him to be.

Of course, this book is written to emphasize the power of the arts for church ministry with a specific focus on dance. Spirit-led movement can give flesh and blood to the bones of holistic faith when a Christ-follower fuses mind, body, and spirit to glorify God through biblical lifestyle choices, by watching that integration in a dance, or by embodying biblical truth as a dancer. Non-verbal movement is the language that provides the connection between the body, worship, and ministry using communication that no one needs to translate. In a profound way, the body speaks when it glorifies and worships God. That is the intent of a Creator God who loves His people and wants them to fully function according to His design. Mark 12:30 reads, "Love the Lord your God

---

[8] Jeremy Begbie, *Beholding the Glory: Incarnation Through the Arts* (Grand Rapids, MI: Baker Academic, 2000), xiii. Fair use.

with all your heart and with all your soul and with all your mind and with all your strength." Of course, to glorify God and to worship Him assumes that we know what those words mean and that we want to become verb followers.

Giving Glory to God

In the Old Testament, glory reflects the idea of "greatness and splendor." In the New Testament, the word translated glory means "dignity, honor, praise, and worship." The writers at gotquestions.org explain, "Putting the two together, we find that glorifying God means to acknowledge His greatness and to give Him honor by praising and worshiping Him, primarily because He, and He alone, deserves to be praised, honored, and worshiped. God's glory is the essence of His nature, and we give glory to Him by recognizing that essence."[9] So glorifying God means that we acknowledge Him as the foundation for our identity and our choices.

The Bible provides numerous examples of the glory God deserves:

> *"Holy, holy, holy is the LORD Almighty; the whole earth is full of his glory" (Isaiah 6:3).*

> *"I am the LORD; that is my name! I will not yield my glory to another or my praise to idols" (Isaiah 42:8).*

> *"Ascribe to the LORD, all you families of nations, ascribe to the LORD glory and strength. Ascribe to the LORD the glory due his name" (1 Chronicles 16:28-29).*

The end result of a verb-based life and dance ministry should always give glory to God. Otherwise, there's no reason for lifestyle movement or dance ministry. This diagram[10] depicts God's original intent for dance:

---

[9] www.gotquestions.org/glorify-God.html. Used with permission.

[10] Jon Lewis, conversation with personal friend, December 2001. Used with permission.

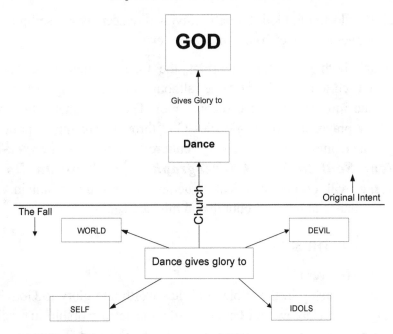

The diagram shows that God's original intention was to use dance to glorify Him because all things were perfectly created by God to honor Him. When the fall occurred, it corrupted that perfection so that humanity and all of creation became a shadow of their original beauty. Author and choreographer Ann Stevenson agrees. "We have allowed our perception and decisions concerning the dance to be shaped and molded by the world's standard."[11]

Instead of glorifying God, sin corrupted dance to glorify the devil, the world, idols, and the self, consistently distorting dance from God's original intent. On the other hand, the church serves to direct God's people to use dance for its intended purpose. It is the job of the church and the mission of the Christian dance community to help the world rediscover God's original intent for dance in two ways:

1. By glorifying God through dancers who use Spirit-led movement to communicate living water in ministry settings.

---

[11] Ann Stevenson, *Restoring Dance* (Shippensburg, PA: Destiny Image Publishers, 1998), 21.

2. By glorifying God through individual dancers who use Spirit-led movements of everyday life to be *verbs*.

Although both goals are important, the focus of this book will be primarily used to cover the first one (although the leadership section will discuss the importance of the second one). The pages that follow will show how prayer-in-motion glorifies God through worship to pour out living water into the 21st-century culture. ***Dance is Prayer-in-Motion: Soul to Sole Choreography for Christian Dance Ministry*** will outline practical structures to set up, maintain, and evaluate a dance ministry in church and ministry settings.

WORSHIP FOR THE SOUL

"Worship is a verb."[12]

The word worship in the Bible attributes worth and glory to God. The meaning of the Hebrew and Greek words translated worship in English are, for the most part, movement words. In the Old Testament, the Hebrew word most commonly used, sahah, means to bow oneself down. In the New Testament, the Greek word used most frequently, proskyneo, means to bow down or prostrate and to kiss. To worship God means that Father, Son, and Spirit are the motivation and the object for our words and actions. Its focus is the condition of the heart. It is not concerned with a particular physical location but rather cuts into the lifestyle people lead. The more we worship the one true God in our life dance, the more we resemble Him. In essence, worship is a declaration of dependence upon Him—akin to a permanent tattoo. We're marked with a living faith that shapes everyday movements.

But the Lord Jesus gave us even more to think about when He personally defined worship: "Yet a time is coming and has now come when the true worshipers will worship the Father in the spirit and in truth, for they are the kind of worshipers the Father seeks. God is spirit, and his worshipers must worship in the spirit and in truth" (John 4:23-24). So true worshipers are to give glory to the Father in spirit and in truth. What

---

[12] Robert Webber, *Worship Is a Verb: Celebrating God's Mighty Deeds of Salvation* (Nashville: Star Song Publishing, 2006). Used with permission from the Webber family.

do those phrases mean?

Worship in Spirit

Spirit: pneuma, primarily denotes "the wind," "breath," and "life"; the spirit is invisible, immaterial, and powerful.[13] When I am told to worship God in spirit and in truth, Holy Spirit-led worship engages my spirit; my spirit refers to the place where God dwells inside of me. My body becomes God's home. Every day I must tune my heart to know God and to listen to His voice: intentionally, unguarded, undistracted, and fully engaged. As I embrace Him with child-like trust and walk in His ways, Abba Father's heart enfolds my heart. Second Corinthians 1:21-22 says, "He anointed us, set his seal of ownership on us, and put his Spirit in our hearts as a deposit, guaranteeing what is to come." Worship "in spirit" enables a holy lifestyle, separated to God, which provides freedom from the bondage of sin.

"Therefore, if anyone is in Christ, the new creation has come. The old has gone, the new is here!" (2 Corinthians 5:17)

On the other hand, without relying on the Holy Spirit to guide my worship, my heart leads my soul to worship me and my desires—and I can be sinful. Money, power, position, and even dance ministry can lead me into idolatry. Many times, either at church or at home, I'm too busy, too worried, too tired, and/or too tempted to surrender my body, mind, and spirit into the arms of Christ.

In his book, *Let the Nations Be Glad,* John Piper said, "When the heart is far from God, worship is vain, empty, nonexistent. The experience of the heart is the defining, vital, indispensable, essence of worship."[14]

---

[13] *Vine's Expository Dictionary of Biblical Words,* Copyright © 1985 by Thomas Nelson Publishers.

[14] John Piper, *Let the Nations Be Glad* (Grand Rapids, MI: Baker Academic, 2003), 219. Fair use.

Worship in Truth

Truth: Conformity to fact or actuality; faithfulness to an original or to a standard;[15] aletheia objectively, signifying "the reality lying at the basis of an appearance; the manifested, veritable essence of a matter."[16]   And what does it mean to worship God in truth? Truth is reality as revealed in Scripture, led by the Spirit, and embodied by Jesus. Not only did Christ maintain that He was the truth (John 14:6), but He also incorporated several forms of the word to reinforce that view. Scripture actually records Jesus speaking the word true 13 times; He repeated the phrase "I tell you the truth" 77 times and often used, "truly, truly" as a prelude to teaching. The phrase "I am" was spoken more than 100 times by Jesus in the New Testament. It was synonymous with His identity as the God of Truth recorded in both the Old and New Testaments.

Therefore, submission of my will to God's is critical to true worship. When I'm a committed verb, my movements (in addition to my thinking, my feelings, and my words) attach themselves to God's ways instead of my own. But it's always my choice. In His kindness, He convicts me when I create my own combinations rather than dance on His pathway (More on this in Chapter 2). To help believers, the Lord Jesus modeled continuous worship to God in spirit and in truth. I like to think of it as prayer-in-motion (PIM).

Have you ever noticed how much people enjoyed being around Jesus? They wanted to share a meal, take a walk, have a lingering conversation, maybe even choreograph a dance. Let's explore why:

1.   For Jesus, worship was not the means to encounter God but emerged from an encounter with God.

2.   For Jesus, worship involved lifestyle not just words.

3.   For Jesus, worship reflected a surrendered heart, not a ritual.

---

[15] Taken from *Nelson's Illustrated Bible Dictionary* edited by Dr. Ronald Youngblood and F.F. Bruce.

Copyright © 1986 by Thomas Nelson Publishers. Used by permission of Thomas Nelson.

www.thomasnelson.com. All rights reserved.

[16] *Vine's Dictionary.*

4. For Jesus, worship expressed a relationship with God, not a search for God.

For Jesus, worship engaged a variety of forms, including song, prayer, Scripture, giving, fasting, and more.[17] "True religion is removed from diet and days, from garments and ceremonies, and placed where it belongs—in the union of the spirit of man with the Spirit of God."[18]

The choice to worship Jesus in spirit and in truth initiates pools of living water. Courage replaces fear. Humility drives us away from pride, and we embrace a life marked by love, compassion, forgiveness, and mercy. Miraculously, as true worshipers, we begin to live and move like Jesus from the inside out. Suddenly, trained dancers and congregational dancers fade into believers who reflect true worship to a living God. And then, in a corporate forum on a Sunday morning, we use an art form like dance to invite others to do the same.

So dance in ministry should be worship, reflect worship, and communicate the gospel from soul to sole—inner movements connecting the heart and mind to the body. Inside to outside. Glorifying God in worship. Communicating truth. Authored and led by the Spirit. We are dancing water. And we have the Source of living water, encouraging us as He sovereignly controls our lives.

Remember, dance is God's idea. That's why it's not surprising that Scripture is full of references to worship, indicating movement beyond sahah and proskyneo (see footnote 19 for number source of Greek and Hebrew words):

1 machowl (maw-khole'); 4234/derived from chuwl 2342; a (round) dance (Psalm 149:3; 150:4; Jeremiah 31:13; Lamentations 5:15)

2 raqad (raw-kad'); 7540; a primitive root; properly, to stamp, i.e. to spring about (wildly or for joy): KJV-dance, jump, leap, skip (1 Chronicles 15:29; Job 21:11; Ecclesiastes 3:4)

---

[17] David Timms, "Lecture on Worship," (lecture, Hope International University, Fullerton, CA, June 8, 2005).

[18] A. W. Tozer, *Man: The Dwelling Place of God* (Camp Hill, PA: Wingspread Publishers, 1966), 4. Used with permission.

3   chagag (khaw-gag'); a primitive root; 2287; properly, to move in a circle, i.e. (specifically) to march in a sacred procession, to observe a festival; by implication, to be giddy. KJV-celebrate, dance, (keep, hold) a (solemn) feast (holiday), reel to and fro (Leviticus 23:41; 1 Samuel 30:16; Psalm 42:4)

4   halal (haw-lal'); 1984; a primitive root; to be clear (orig. of sound, but usually of color); to shine; hence, to make a show, to boast; and thus to be (clamorously) foolish; to rave; causatively, to celebrate; also to stultify: KJV-(make) boast (self), celebrate, commend, (deal, make), fool (-ish, -ly), glory, give [light], be (make, feignself) mad (against), give in marriage, [sing, be worthy of] praise, rage, renowned, shine (1 Chronicles 23:5; Psalm 135:1; 149:3; 150:4)

5   karar (kaw-rar'); 3769; a primitive root; to dance (i.e. whirl): - dance (-ing) (2 Samuel 6:14, 16)

6   chuwl (khool); or chiyl (kheel); 2342; a primitive root; properly, to twist or whirl (in a circular or spiral manner), i.e. (specifically) to dance, to writhe in pain (especially of parturition) or fear; figuratively, to wait, to pervert: KJV-bear, (make to) bring forth, (make to) calve, dance, drive away, fall grievously (with pain), fear, form, great, grieve, (be) grievous, hope, look, make, be in pain, be much (sore) pained, rest, shake, shapen, (be) sorrow (-ful), stay, tarry, travail (with pain), tremble, trust, wait carefully (patiently), be wounded (Judges 21:21, 23)

7   rejoice:

    a. OT: 1523 giyl (gheel); or (by permutation) guwl (gool); a primitive root; properly, to spin round (under the influence of any violent emotion), i.e. usually rejoice, or (as cringing) fear: KJV-be glad, joy, be joyful, rejoice (1 Chronicles 16:31; Psalm 97:1)

    b. OT: 5970 `alats (aw-lats'); a primitive root; to jump for joy, i.e. exult: KJV-be joyful, rejoice, triumph (Psalm 9:2; 68:3)

c. NT: 4640 skirtao (skeer-tah'-o); akin to skairo (to skip); to jump, i.e. sympathetically move (as the quickening of a fetus): KJV-leap (for joy) (Luke 1:41, 44; 6:23)

d. OT: 8055 samach (saw-makh'); a primitive root; probably to brighten up, i.e. (figuratively) be (causatively, make) blithe or gleesome: KJV-cheer up, be (make) glad, (have, make) joy (-ful), be (make) merry, (cause to, make to) rejoice, very. (Deuteronomy 12:12; 2 Chronicles 20:27; Job 21:12; Zephaniah 3:14)

e. NT: 21 agalliao (ag-al-lee-ah'-o); from agan (much) and NT:242; properly, to jump for joy, i.e. exult: KJV-be (exceeding) glad, with exceeding joy, rejoice (greatly) (John 5:35; 1 Peter 1:6,8 4:13)

8   no`am; (no-am) 5278: kindness, pleasantness, delightfulness, beauty, favor (Psalm 27:4-6; 90:17) [19]

With all these words to increase our understanding, let's read some Bible verses that highlight movement and dance.

In Psalms, we read:

"Come, let us bow down in worship, let us kneel before the LORD our Maker" (Psalm 95:6)

"Worship the LORD in the splendor of his holiness; tremble before him, all the earth" (Psalm 96:9)

"Lift up your hands in the sanctuary and praise the LORD" (Psalm 134:2)

"May my prayer be set before you like incense; may the lifting up of my hands be like the evening sacrifice" (Psalm 141:2)

---

[19] *Biblesoft's New Exhaustive Strong's Numbers and Concordance with Expanded Greek-Hebrew Dictionary* (Seattle, WA: Biblesoft, Inc and International Bible Translators, Inc), software. Bible verses added by author.

"Let Israel rejoice in their Maker; let the people of Zion be glad in their King. Let them praise his name with dancing and make music to him with timbrel and harp" (Psalm 149:2-3)

"Praise him with timbrel and dancing, praise him with the strings and pipe, praise him with the clash of cymbals, praise him with resounding cymbals. Let everything that has breath praise the LORD" (Psalm 150:4-6)

Other Old Testament references to movement are:

"When all the people saw this, they fell prostrate and cried, 'The LORD—he is God! The LORD—he is God!'"(1 Kings 18:39)

"Elijah . . . bent down to the ground and put his face between his knees" (1 Kings 18:42)

"All the men of Judah, with their wives and children and little ones, stood there before the Lord . . . . Jehoshaphat bowed down with his face to the ground, and all the people . . . fell down in worship before the LORD" (2 Chronicles 20:13, 18-19).

"Solomon stood before the altar of the LORD in front of the whole assembly of Israel, spread out his hands towards heaven and said: 'LORD, the God of Israel'" (1 Kings 8:22-23)

"When Pharaoh's horses, chariots and horsemen went into the sea, the LORD brought the waters of the sea back over them, but the Israelites walked through the sea on dry ground. Then Miriam the prophet, Aaron's sister, took a timbrel in her hand, and all the women followed her, with timbrels and dancing. Miriam sang to them: 'Sing to the LORD, for he is highly exalted. Both horse and driver, he has hurled into the sea'" (Exodus 15:19-21)

"When the men were returning home after David had killed the Philistine, the women came out from all the towns of Israel to meet King Saul with singing and dancing, with joyful songs and with timbrels and lyres. As they danced, they sang: 'Saul has

slain his thousands, and David his tens of thousands'" (1 Samuel 18:6-7)

"Wearing a linen ephod, David was dancing before the LORD with all his might, while he and all Israel were bringing up the ark of the LORD with shouts and the sound of trumpets" (2 Samuel 6:14-15)

"Joy is gone from our hearts; our dancing has turned to mourning" (Lamentations 5:15)

"I will build you up again, and you, Virgin Israel, will be rebuilt. Again you will take up your timbrels and go out to dance with the joyful" (Jeremiah 31:4)

"Then young women will dance and be glad, young men and old as well. I will turn their mourning into gladness; I will give them comfort and joy instead of sorrow" (Jeremiah 31:13)

"Rejoice in the LORD and be glad, you righteous; sing, all you who are upright in heart!" (Psalm 32:11)

"Let the sea resound, and all that is in it; let the fields be jubilant, and everything in them!" (1 Chronicles 16:32)

Here are multiple references to worship, dance, and movement in the New Testament:

"Rejoice in that day and leap for joy" (Luke 6:23)

"He withdrew about a stone's throw beyond them, knelt down and prayed" (Luke 22:41)

"When he had led them out to the vicinity of Bethany, he lifted up his hands and blessed them" (Luke 24:50)

"She began to wet [Jesus'] feet with her tears. Then she wiped them with her hair, kissed them and poured perfume on them" (Luke 7:38)

"I kneel before the Father, from whom his whole family in heaven and on earth derives its name" (Ephesians 3:14-15)

"At the name of Jesus every knee should bow" (Philippians 2:10)

"I want men everywhere to pray, lifting up holy hands, without anger or disputing" (1Timothy 2:8)

"After this I looked, and there before me was a great multitude that no one could count, from every nation, tribe, people and language, standing before the throne and before the Lamb. They were wearing white robes and were holding palm branches in their hands . . . . All the angels were standing around the throne and around the elders and the four living creatures. They fell down on their faces before the throne and worshiped God" (Revelation 7:9, 11)

"In all this you greatly rejoice, though now for a little while you may have had to suffer grief in all kinds of trials" (1 Peter 1:6)

These verses (and many more) demonstrate how worship and movement blend together to give glory to God. That's why it has been helpful for me to identify different categories of worship for a potential dance project. Although evaluation takes thought, this understanding adds one more layer to the dance ministry process that results in clear choreography. The worship categories I use for movement are:

1. PRAISE: As a reflection of what it means to be a "living sacrifice" and "a holy temple" by modeling a variety of biblical responses.

2. BEAUTY: As a visual, sensory vehicle for restoration and healing, providing renewal to a worshiper through the mystery of the Holy Spirit.

3. TEACHING: As a learning and evangelistic tool, accessing the creative imagination through communication of biblical concepts that use truth, story, and symbol.

4. CELEBRATION: As a conduit to build the unity of the Church through community celebration.

5. PRAYER: As a direct avenue to speak with God using movement in the form of supplication, meditation, intercession, or protection from the power of Satan.

"Movement without the involvement of our hearts and minds does not constitute worship. Movement in ritual may become habitual and empty. This can also be true of the words that we pray. In answering one of the teachers of the law, Jesus said that the most important commandment was to love God with every part of you."[20]

SOUL TO SOLE MOVEMENT: PRAYER-IN-MOTION

Let's review. Earlier we learned that God sculpted the body to be good and designed it to glorify Him in worship. We also realized the body speaks as a potent communication vehicle. If this is God's intent, why has the Church been reluctant to use dance as a viable means of worship within the Christian community? Perhaps one reason for the weakness in this area is that human beings have a tendency to compartmentalize faith. Sometimes we love God with our minds but cut off our feelings and/or our bodies as we worship Him. On the other hand, sometimes we allow feelings to lead faith without the transformation of the mind.

Either choice can produce segmented beliefs and actions that don't beckon the secular world to a personal faith in Jesus (See Chapter 2). Then, too, the secular culture signals a distorted misuse of the body by using it in perverted ways. That frightens people. But we are not called to make decisions out of fear: ***"For the Spirit God gave us does not make us timid, but gives us power, love and self-discipline" (2 Timothy 1:7).*** Christ-followers are called to use God's good gifts in appropriate ways that glorify His name.

---

[20] Mary Jones, *God's People on the Move* (Australia: Christian Dance Fellowship of Australia, 1988), 11. Used with permission.

With a body designed for worship and communication by a loving God, where are they? Where are the Christian dancers in the Church? Where is the dance ministry training to support all the visual conversation out there? There are plenty of Christian dancers using their gifts for secular purposes. On the other hand, like all other art forms, we need Christian dancers to maximize their gifts inside the Church. There are a few Christian dance companies and there are a few on-going church dance ministries, but they can't begin to fill the void that we see nationally. And most dance ministries do not last.

Reasons Why

Let's briefly look at the reasons why dance has not been effectively implemented in a church and ministry context. Here are the facts:

1. Many pastors are unfamiliar with dance movement in church ministry settings as dance has not traditionally been incorporated into many church ministries. Even if pastors wanted to incorporate movement ministry into worship, there are few resources available to them- particularly resources that might help them to evaluate dance success or failure.

2. We have pastors and congregants who feel uncomfortable with the use of the body as a means of worship. Their discomfort is often based on unbiblical teaching in the past and/or present examples of inappropriate dance.

3. We have a vast group of trained and congregational dancers from professional to beginning ranks who reflect a variety of problems hindering their effectiveness in dance ministry: lack of unity in theology as well as training, weak choreography, poor music choice, lack of practical ministry structures and inappropriate clothing and/or movement choices.

Sole to Sole or Soul to Sole?

Is there a difference between secular dance and Christian dance? Is all Christian dance appropriate for church/ministry presentations? Is it possible that we need to develop a specific label for dance in church/ministry settings that adheres to the same criteria that worship and teaching pastors in a Sunday morning service seek to demonstrate? If so, what would that be?

To understand the challenges associated with dance in Christendom, let's untangle the confusion by defining some terms:

Dance: Rhythmic movement of the feet or body, usually set to music (Webster's Dictionary).

Remember that dance expresses ideas in a universal, non-verbal language that often "speaks" as powerfully as spoken language. That makes a strong case for using dance to communicate the gospel in ministry settings. But not all dance is Christian dance. And not all Christian dance targets a clear, biblical message.

Think through what it means to embody living water. Although Christian dance would fall under the definition of dance from secular eyes, it includes "verb" criteria, which secular dance artists would not tolerate or care about. But we need to care because God cares. Let's look at how Christian dance would differ from the definition of secular dance.

Christian dance: Rhythmic movement of the feet or body, usually set to music. Movement used to glorify God.

All Christian dance should use movement to glorify God no matter what dance form is being expressed. These forms include (but are not limited to) spontaneous worship movement within a church service (a.k.a. prophetic dance) along with folk dance, musicals, children's dance, and creative dance, including all styles of dance training (ballet, modern, jazz, hip-hop, tap, etc.), which utilize movements that do not conflict with biblical values.

Often, however, Christian dance reflects no conceptual biblical communication in a worship/ministry setting. In other words, some types of Christian dance do not have specific biblical intent. For example, I have participated in a wide variety of folk dances from many countries. It's fun to use my body to give glory to God in this context. No, it's not a church setting, and there is no reference to biblical themes; but it is Christian dance all the same because it gives glory to God. Of course, the same thing can be true for television and the Internet. When I have seen Big Bird dancing on Sesame Street, it makes me smile. I think God is smiling too because He sees Himself glorified in the movement. What this means is that you don't have to go to church to enjoy a wide variety of Christian dance. This is true of music and art as well. It might be that a non-Christian choreographer creates a dance that gives glory to God without having that intention. After all, God's creatures are made in His image and all of us reflect His glory indirectly.

Of course, you must evaluate the dance movement that you watch, and you must discern whether it gives glory to God. If it doesn't, avoid that setting or that theater or that dance studio. More important, there are situations where the presentation of Christian dance should go deeper in its intent. There is a noticeable difference between a folk dance or a ballet that gives glory to God outside a church ministry setting, and a Christian dance that is presented inside a church or ministry context with a clear conceptual message.

Prayer-in-motion (PIM) is the label I use for choreographed, Spirit-led dance that targets a biblical concept in a worship setting. The Spirit-led dance needs to be intentional in what it communicates because people come to ministry/church settings to deepen their faith, learn about Jesus, and worship corporately. A gifted singer cannot sing "She'll Be Coming Around the Mountain" in church on Sunday morning even though the voice and the song may give glory to God. A gifted speaker cannot preach on the history of the Roman Empire even though the text of the talk is inspiring. A gifted dancer cannot dance a solo from Swan Lake during a Sunday morning worship service even though it is a beautiful ballet. Just as a preaching pastor and a music pastor must choose what they say and sing in intentional ways when they share their gifts in a ministry context, a dance ministry with a choreographed dance needs to do the same thing. PIM clarifies the difference between a Christian dance that gives glory to God and a Christian dance that glorifies God in worship by communicating a specific biblical concept. Below is a further definition of PIM.

Prayer-in-motion:
1.   *Rhythmic movement of the feet or body, usually set to music.*

2.   *Soul to Sole Choreography used to glorify God in worship which captures praise, beauty, teaching, celebration, and/or prayer.*

3.   *Soul to Sole Choreography used to glorify God that identifies a biblical, conceptual target during church services and ministry situations.*

4.   *Dancers embodying sensory movement using mind, body, and spirit given fully to the Lord Jesus.*

5.   *Transformation of dance movement into ministry.*

Now let's clarify what prayer-in-motion is not:

1.   PIM is not random "feelings" expressed in isolation from biblical truth.

2.   PIM is not a series of dance movements done at the same time a Christian song is played.

3.   PIM is not a performance-oriented show with a focus on technical skills.

Prayer-in-Motion: Worship with Conceptual, Targeted Choreography

According to Webster's Dictionary, concept is defined as: an idea, a thought, a general notion.

Although all dance is movement, it is not necessarily Christian dance. If it is Christian dance, it contains movement that glorifies God but does not always belong in a church/ministry setting. PIM not only intentionally gives glory to God through worship movement, but it also presents an identified conceptual biblical concept and communicates that target. That is why the definition of PIM is important to the development of choreography. And that's why the Soul to Sole Choreography method facilitates the creative process for ministry settings. It enables dancers, choreographers, and church staff to frame, understand, and evaluate PIM using effective criteria. As we will see later on in this book, Soul to Sole Choreography structures preview into any dance prior to choreography creation and presentation. It's a safety valve for dancers, choreographers, congregations, and pastors.

The bottom line is this: The foundation for Soul to Sole Choreography that produces PIM should include at least one identified worship category and one biblical conceptual target for each dance considered for ministry presentation (This method is outlined in Chapter 4).

Mission of Prayer-in-Motion

The mission of Christian dance should be to give glory to God. However, the mission of PIM is more specific: (1) It uses planned movement (Soul to Sole Choreography) as an expression of worship (praise, beauty, teaching, celebration, prayer) to glorify God during church services and ministry situations with (2) a specific choreography concept and song/text that communicates a biblical, conceptual message.

Vision for Prayer-in-Motion

A vision statement for PIM guides dancers, choreographers, congregations, and pastors into a biblical understanding of reasons why dance should be used to share the gospel:

"Within the church/ministries of Jesus Christ, PIM should be used as an expression of faith for worship to bring glory to a Holy God through heart transformation of the people viewing the presentation."

"The arts can tell us the experiential truth about spiritual reality."[21]

The worship movement presented in church settings should be "living water" designed to follow the Holy Spirit as He draws unsaved and saved people to Him in transformative ways (including dancers in the rehearsal process). If we are faithful to communicate biblical truth within society at large, PIM has an opportunity to present the gospel of Jesus Christ through dance. We have powerful, non-verbal communication tools to use that no other art form can enlist. The tools, which reflect the Master Choreographer, need to be carefully and delicately handled.

The 21st century does not acknowledge the wonder of transcendent truth. The secular mind does not glorify God or seek to know Him. More than ever, PIM can be used to remind the Church of the hope we have in

---

[21] Leland Ryken, *The Liberated Imagination: Thinking Christianly About the Arts* (Wheaton, IL: Harold Shaw Publishers, 1989), 139.

Christ while non-believers can see the invitation of Christ in a way that challenges purposeless thinking. Secular art reflects what secular culture values: a lack of transcendent truth. Christian art reflects what Christian culture values: unchanging, transcendent truth.

"Show me your ways, LORD, teach me your paths. Guide me in your truth and teach me, for you are God my Savior, and my hope is in you all day long" (Psalm 25:4-5)

"The Christian artist is, ideally, the speaker for the Christian view of things in the world of the arts and in society. If the Christian church extends its hands of blessing and support over its missionaries of the gospel, should it not do the same for those who speak the truth through art to an unbelieving world?"[22]

---

[22] Ryken, 216.

Chapter 2

Leadership:
Passion from the Soul to the Sole

Passion: strong love (Webster's Dictionary)

Soon after our engagement, my fiancé Richard introduced me to one of the great passions of his life: donuts. To be specific, he opened my eyes to enjoy cake ones loaded with sprinkles, icing, and all kinds of sweet goo. For many years, I've investigated the fine nuances of what makes a donut melt in your mouth by trekking to all of the area donut stores. And when I bite into a fresh donut, I know whether it's the real thing or not.

But that's not my passion. My passion is fruit. A few weeks ago, I meandered into a local restaurant and ordered the specialty of the house: tropical fruit tea. I watched the server shake it with gusto. He took about 1/3 cup of tea, squeezed in two fresh oranges, added a slice of lemon, and crumbled in some mint. Ahhh. No mistaking real fruit in that concoction.

There's nothing like the real thing. On the other hand, there's nothing as disappointing as false advertising, especially when you can taste the difference between the real thing and the imitation. Authentic faith in Jesus works in the same way. It results in a bona fide, unmistakable taste for loving God and others. It also produces the fruit of the spirit: "love, joy, peace, forbearance, kindness, goodness, faithfulness, gentleness and self-control" (Galatians 5:22-23). But when man-made ingredients get into the mix, the result lacks authentic flavor.

"Many Christians have wandered into a spiritual wilderness devoid of passion and power. Those who hear and obey the voice

of God will escape that wilderness or even see it changed into a garden."[23]

When I was a young girl, I had a wilderness mentality. I assumed I was a Christian because I went to church and participated in its social activities. I assumed I knew God. I didn't know that God's home belonged inside my body. I didn't know that I didn't know about a personal relationship with Jesus. I didn't know that I didn't know how to listen to Him. I didn't know about a fallen world and the effects of sin. And I thought the reality of Satan was a joke.

When I worshiped God in form rather than content, I timed prayers on Sunday mornings and thought communion was boring because it made the service take too long. During the week, I thought nothing was wrong with a bad attitude or an unloving heart. Most of the time, I was unaware of what I projected to others. If I didn't like somebody, conflict was my time to "win" with reactive responses. And, of course, I didn't "get" love. I thought I had to feel loving to be loving. So each day was a reaction to how I felt. In that context, I was the authority in my life, and I saw Jesus as the assistant who agreed with my daily agenda and my definition of truth. Yet, my faith had no power.

Looking back through my brokenness, I see how sinful and self-oriented I was. By the grace of God, I began to worship God "in spirit and in truth" by renewing my mind with His mind (Romans 12:1-2). My self-talk changed from condemnation to gentle conviction. Internal self-awareness helped me to agree with transcendent truth as God wrote His ways on my heart from the inside out—soul to sole. These experiences profoundly affected my personal choices and transformed my attitudes so that I morphed into a new person. Passion for Jesus took me from "walking in the flesh" to "walking in the Spirit." Second Corinthians 5:17 even says, "Therefore, if anyone is in Christ, the new creation has come. The old has gone, the new is here!"

As time went on, I realized the way my daily life reflected love through obedience to God demonstrated the practical reality of faith in Christ. I

---

[23] Taken from *Surprised by the Voice of God* by Jack Deere, Copyright © 1996. Used by permission of Zondervan. www.zondervan.com.

was learning a "new way to be human." [24] So what's the point? For God to use you and me effectively as leaders in dance ministry, we must agree with His way of doing things. We are not the ultimate authority in our lives. The Lord Jesus is. And He has sent the Helper, the Holy Spirit, to fill us with the power to do His will. We can't assume we know God's will or His ways. We can't assume we will do His will. In fact, we can't assume anything.

ASSUMPTIONS: EXTERNAL FORM VS. INTERNAL CONTENT

Most of us live on unreliable assumptions. For instance, I assume that if I buy a coffee pot at the store (the form), it will work; but that's not necessarily true. I find out if it's true when the coffee pot perks and produces coffee (the content) consistently.

As a young married couple, my husband and I bought a new house and assumed it was well built (the form). That wasn't true either. We had to replace the air conditioning, the roof, and the flooring as well as other aspects of the house soon after we moved in (the content). We're still reaping the consequences of house form that did not match house content. According to statistical data compiled by George Barna, the views of faith held by born-again Christians were not significantly different from those of other adults. The details indicated "less than one out of every ten church attenders spends any time during a typical week worshiping God, other than when they are at a church service."

In fact, widespread confusion regarding purpose, meaning, and truth has ravaged the core of many churches. Many adults believe they know all the basic teachings of Christianity. But when they explore what they think the Bible actually teaches, many theological inconsistencies and inaccuracies emerge between what they believe and what the Bible says. [25]

---

[24] Taken from *The Challenge of Jesus* by N.T. Wright. Copyright (c) 1999 by N. T. Wright. Used by permission of InterVarsity Press, P.O. Box 1400, Downers Grove, IL 60515, USA. www.ivpress.com

[25] George Barna, www.barna.org/barna-update/article/5-barna-update/166-barna-reviews-top-religious-trends-of-2005?q=worship+confusion and www.barna.org/barna-update/article/5-barna-update/87-barna-identifies-seven-paradoxes-regarding-americas-faith?q=worship+confusion.

Jesus noticed the same problem in the Jewish leadership He came to serve. Their faith had weak content. "These people honor me with their lips, but their hearts are far from me. They worship me in vain; their teachings are merely human rules" (Matthew 15:8-9). We make a mistake by assuming that we produce fruit for Christ because we go to church or lead a ministry or dance to Christian music. This assumption often creates churches, dance ministries, and dance leaders that can mirror form rather than content.

> *"A little bit of the Bible doesn't help and doesn't change lives; it is the repeated workouts over a period of months, even years, that dramatically changes you."*[26]

> *"Concern for appearance might be the original American sin. The temptation to settle for looking good while everything else is falling apart inside can be dangerous. After a long season of accepting appearance for reality, a Christian forgets what truth even sounds like."*[27]

In leadership, how do we produce a dance ministry that develops passion-filled, fruit-based content rather than external form? Jesus told us how to do it: "Apart from me you can do nothing" (John 15:5). That sounds like an obvious focus for choreography and rehearsal but honestly, it's easy to forget Jesus in the process of ministry. Let's counteract that possibility by investing in three combinations that will keep us out of the wilderness and grow a garden in dance leadership: know God, listen to God, and love God and others.

THREE COMBINATIONS FOR DEVELOPING LEADERSHIP CONTENT

"For in him we live and move and have our being" (Acts 17:28).

Leadership Combo A: Know God Intentionally

Frederica Mathewes-Green said, "Being 'in Christ'; it is a transforming condition; it means the life of Jesus himself is within you, illuminating

---

[26] Deere, 105.

[27] Brennan Manning, *The Relentless Tenderness* (Grand Rapids, MI: Fleming H. Revell, 2004), 116. Fair use.

you. This is the calling of every Christian; the process is called theosis which means that one's essential being is permeated and filled with the presence of God. It is something more than merely resembling Jesus, more than merely following. It is transformation."[28]

With theosis leading the way, take time each day to kindle and deepen friendship with God. Know God on purpose. Don't hope it will happen. Make it happen. Start by evaluating your schedule right now. Look at the actions that occur in your daily life. The actions you choose will expose you to what you really value (TV, food, friends, sports, etc.). Is there time for Jesus? To be an effective leader, add God to your priority list and bring Him into your real life, not just your church life. This is because intimacy with God depends on personal choice (James 4:8). Remember, you can't represent someone you don't know, and you can't lead others where you haven't been. Make knowing Jesus a central thing.

I often pray, study, read, and meditate on Scripture in the mornings, listen to CDs in the car (and other times), involve myself in Bible studies, and/or memorize Scripture. I invest in godly relationships—women who challenge me to grow like Jesus. I also change my routine from year to year. But don't copy me. Just make sure that you spend time with God on a regular basis so that you renew your mind with His mind (Romans 12:2, James 4:8).

It might also help to know that in Scripture, the word set is a synonym for decision-based intentionality. We are to set our hope, set our minds, and set our hearts on Jesus—knowing that the truth will set us free. Romans 8:5 says, "Those who live according to the flesh have their minds *set* on what the flesh desires; but those who live in accordance with the Spirit have their minds set on what the Spirit desires" (italics added).

---

[28] *The Illumined Heart* by Frederica Mathewes-Green, Copyright © 2001 by Frederica Mathewes-Green. Used with permission of www.paracletepress.com.

Leadership Combo B: Listen to God

"We must learn to soundproof the heart against the intruding noises of the public world in order to hear what God has to say."[29]

Enter into the quiet with Jesus and expect Him to speak. A chaotic, too-busy life hinders the pathway to listening (See Appendix A for practical steps to implement Combinations A and B).

Psalm 37:7 says, "Be still before the LORD and wait patiently for him." Don't allow your relationship with the Lord to be one sided. Jesus created relationships with Him to communicate reciprocally: back and forth. If God listens to me and I don't listen to Him, the relationship ceases to be intimate. And Scripture confirms that Jesus planned a conversational relationship with His people.

John 10:27 says, "My sheep listen to my voice; I know them, and they follow me."

Isaiah 28:23 says, "Listen and hear my voice; pay attention and hear what I say."

Mother Teresa, the nun who won the Nobel Peace Prize for her work with the poor, articulates this idea beautifully: "The essential thing is not what we say, but what God says to us and through us. All our words will be useless unless they come from within—words which do not give the light of Christ increase the darkness." This applies to our movements as well.

Leadership Combo C: Love God and Others

"Walk in the way of love" (Ephesians 5:2).

Love for God produces love for others. Respond with God's heart to friends and enemies. Without a clear understanding of biblical love and your own inner motivations, it becomes easy to misunderstand the purpose for ministry leadership.

---

[29] Gordon MacDonald, Taken from *Ordering Your Private World* by Gordon MacDonald. Copyright © 1985.

Used by permission of Thomas Nelson. www.thomasnelson.com. All rights reserved.

Look at Bible verses that challenge leaders to love others as Jesus did:

"A new command I give you: Love one another. As I have loved you, so you must love one another. By this everyone will know that you are my disciples, if you love one another" (John 13:34-35).

"Love your enemies, do good to those who hate you, bless those who curse you, pray for those who mistreat you" (Luke 6:27-28).

"Now that you have purified yourselves by obeying the truth so that you have sincere love for each other, love one another deeply, from the heart. For you have been born again, not of perishable seed, but of imperishable, through the living and enduring word of God" (1 Peter 1:22-23).

"Dear friends, let us love one another, for love comes from God. Everyone who loves has been born of God and knows God. Whoever does not love does not know God, because God is love" (1 John 4:7-8).

"Above all, love each other deeply, because love covers over a multitude of sins" (1 Peter 4:8).

"We put no stumbling block in anyone's path, so that our ministry will not be discredited. Rather, as servants of God we commend ourselves in every way: in great endurance; in troubles, hardships and distresses; in beatings, imprisonments and riots; in hard work, sleepless nights and hunger; in purity, understanding, patience and kindness; in the Holy Spirit and in sincere love; in truthful speech and in the power of God; with weapons of righteousness in the right hand and in the left" (2 Corinthians 6:3-7).

"Love must be sincere. Hate what is evil; cling to what is good. Be devoted to one another in brotherly love. Honor one another above yourselves. Never be lacking in zeal, but keep your spiritual fervor, serving the Lord. Be joyful in hope, patient in

affliction, faithful in prayer. Share with the Lord's people who are in need. Practice hospitality" (Romans 12:9-13).

"Do not repay anyone evil for evil. Be careful to do what is right in the eyes of everyone. If it is possible, as far as it depends on you, live at peace with everyone" (Romans 12:17-18).

"You have heard that it was said, 'Love your neighbor and hate your enemy.' But I tell you, love your enemies and pray for those who persecute you, that you may be children of your Father in heaven. He causes his sun to rise on the evil and the good, and sends rain on the righteous and the unrighteous. If you love those who love you, what reward will you get? Are not even the tax collectors doing that? And if you greet only your own people, what are you doing more than others? Do not even pagans do that? Be perfect, therefore, as your heavenly Father is perfect" (Matthew 5:43-48).

We love because he first loved us. If anyone says, 'Whoever claims to love god, yet hates a brother or sister is a liar. For whoever does not love their brother and sister, whom they have seen, cannot love God, whom they have not seen. And he has given us this command: Anyone who loves God must also love their brother and sister" (1 John 4:19-21).

"Instead, speaking the truth in love, we will grow to become in every respect the mature body of him who is the head, that is, Christ" (Ephesians 4:15).

"If I speak in the tongues of men or of angels, but not have love, I am only a resounding gong or a clanging cymbal. If I have the gift of prophecy and can fathom all mysteries and all knowledge, and if I have a faith that can move mountains, but do not have love, I am nothing. If I give all I possess to the poor and give over my body to the hardship that I may boast, but have not love, I gain nothing. Love is patient, love is kind. It does not envy, it does not boast, it is not proud. It does not dishonor others, it is not self-seeking, it is not easily angered, it keeps no record of wrongs.

Love does not delight in evil but rejoices with the truth. It always protects, always trusts, always hopes, always perseveres. Love never fails. But where there are prophecies, they will cease; where there are tongues, they will be stilled; where there is knowledge, it will pass away. For we know in part and we prophesy in part, but when completeness comes, what is in part disappears. When I was a child, I talked like a child, I thought like a child, I reasoned like a child. When I became a man, I put the ways of childhood behind me. For now we see only a reflection as in a mirror; then we shall see face to face. Now I know in part; then I shall know fully, even as I am fully known. And now these three remain: faith, hope and love. But the greatest of these is love" (1 Corinthians 13).

"Brothers and sisters, if someone is caught in a sin, you who live by the Spirit should restore that person gently. But watch yourselves, or you also may be tempted. Carry each other's burdens, and in this way you will fulfill the law of Christ" (Galatians 6:1-2).

"For the kingdom of God is not a matter of talk but of power. What do you prefer? Shall I come to you with a rod of discipline, or shall I come in love and with a gentle spirit?" (1 Corinthians 4:20-21).

"Now this is our boast: Our conscience testifies that we have conducted ourselves in the world, and especially in our relations with you, with integrity and godly sincerity. We have done so, relying not on worldly wisdom but on God's grace" (2 Corinthians 1:12).

DEFINITION OF GOD'S LOVE: AGAPE

"Christian love, whether exercised toward the brethren, or toward men generally, is not an impulse from the feelings, it does not always run with the natural inclinations, nor does it spend itself only upon those for whom some affinity is discovered. Love seeks the welfare of all (Romans 15:2) and works no ill to any (Romans 13:8-10); love seeks opportunity to do good to 'all men, and especially toward them that are of the household of the faith' (Galatians 6:10) (See for further reference: 1 Corinthians 13 and Colossians 3:12-14)."[30]

God's agape love is not the same as human love. Human love is rooted in self-based motives with an emphasis on feelings and performance. The Christ-like love of believers doesn't have to feel loving to be loving. As we get to know God, He transforms our minds, hearts, and bodies to reflect His character. We begin to mirror His ways more than our ways. "It's an unconditional giving of yourself for another with no strings attached. God's Love is a Love that keeps on loving even when the object of that love ceases to please or even tries to stop that Love from coming."[31]

Agape love does not react to people with disrespect. It evaluates its motives first and then listens to the Spirit's leading for direction in all situations. In conflict, it does not ignore difficult circumstances or difficult people; the relational goal should not be to win or to be superior to anyone but to express transcendent truth in a foundation of grace. Authentic biblical love actually translates into obedient choices that grow organic faith content. "And this is love: that we walk in obedience to his commands. As you have heard from the beginning, his command is that you walk in love" (2 John 6).

What is your response to a congregational member who thinks that dance is sin? How do you handle yourself when a dancer comes into rehearsal with a bad attitude? In leadership, you will be tested. Friends and enemies both need a model of Christ-like love. In fact, how you love them reflects your understanding of how God loves you when you are at your best and worst. And to be clear about how to handle the inevitable mix of leadership situations, you will need to know God, listen to God, and love God and others. Remember to plug in to the right power source. "All this I have spoken while still with you. But the Advocate, the Holy Spirit, whom the Father will send in my name, will teach you all things and will remind you of everything I have said to you" (John 14:25-26).

---

[30] *Notes on Thessalonians*, C. F. Hogg and W. E. Vine, 1908-1911, public domain.

[31] Chuck Missler and Nancy Missler, *The Way of Agape* (Coeur d'Alene, ID: The Kings High Way Ministries, Inc, 2001), 41. Used with permission.

The Practical Test of Leadership

1. What is your heart attitude and response to a situation when you don't get your own way and when you know you are right?

2. Do you expose others to the unconditional love of God in situations that frustrate you?

3. Do you still recognize that God is sovereign and that He allows any situation in your life as a way to test your faith and conform your character?

4. When you are dealing with an "enemy," do you ask: "What is wrong with my connection to Christ that I am having trouble loving this person?"

"Bless my enemies O Lord. Even I bless them and do not curse them. Enemies have driven me into your embrace more than friends have. Friends have bound me to earth, enemies have loosed me from earth and have demolished all my aspirations in the world."[32]

LEADERSHIP AND THE ENEMY

Scripture teaches us many important lessons as we deal with enemies. First Peter 1:7 reminds us that enemies both purify and grow our faith as we look to God in trust. Ephesians 6 warns us that Satan is THE enemy who works to unleash strife throughout a fallen world.

"For our struggle is not against flesh and blood, but against the rulers, against the authorities, against the powers of this dark world and against the spiritual forces of evil in the heavenly realms. Therefore put on the full armor of God, so that when the day of evil comes, you may be able to stand your ground, and after you have done everything, to stand. Stand firm then, with the belt of truth buckled around your waist, with the breastplate of righteousness in place, and with your feet fitted with the readiness that comes from the gospel of peace. In addition to all

---

[32] Bishop Nikolai Velimirovic, a Serbian bishop in the 20th century.

this, take up the shield of faith, with which you can extinguish all the flaming arrows of the evil one. Take the helmet of salvation and the sword of the Spirit, which is the word of God. And pray in the Spirit on all occasions with all kinds of prayers and requests. With this in mind, be alert and always keep on praying for all the Lord's people" (Ephesians 6:12-18).

Remember to put on the full armor of God in ministry leadership and don't be surprised by enemy warfare. At times, Satan will engage in internal attacks to tempt you, external attacks to discourage you, and difficult circumstances to weaken you. Fight battles with the Spirit-filled weapons that Scripture describes above and understand that lifestyle worship centered in agape love is the most potent counter-attack against the arrows of the evil one.

Implementation of Agape Leadership: Choices Controlled by the Spirit or the Flesh Choice.

Who's in control of the ministry that you lead? You or Jesus? Do you self-evaluate the motives for your choices so that you implement agape love in your leadership? Remember, the Lord Jesus doesn't force His children to do anything. In fact, the New Testament gives us a specific label for our leadership choices. We can either walk in the Spirit with love as the power base or walk in the flesh with self as the power base.

"So I say, walk by the Spirit, and you will not gratify the desires of the flesh. For the flesh desires what is contrary to the Spirit, and the Spirit what is contrary to the flesh. They are in conflict with each other, so that you are not to do whatever you want. But if you are led by the Spirit, you are not under the law" (Galatians 5:16-18).

In case you're not sure what Scripture means by "led by the flesh" or "led by the spirit," let's clarify. The flesh means to do things your way, with your will, serving your purposes. You. You and your feelings. You and the wilderness. You and your reactions. On the other hand, to be led by the Spirit means to agree to choose God's way of doing things in dance leadership allowing the Holy Spirit to transform and guide you to serve His purposes. The result produces redemptive, agape love.

Honesty about your own personal heart condition allows for choices that lead to garden cultivation. The two lists below demonstrate some of the practical differences between what the flesh wants and what the Spirit desires. The numbers 1-14 on each list correlate with the transformation that occurs when the love of Christ (and obedience) shake up the life of a believer. The list also describes the grace-based changes that occurred in my heart as I began to understand the difference between form and content, flesh and spirit, and wilderness and garden. Remember that sanctification is process-based.

"The thing is to understand myself, to see what God really wishes me to do."[33]

To learn more about walking in the Spirit and to identify additional resources on this topic, consult Appendix B.

---

[33] Soren Kierkegaard, 1813-1855.

World's Perspective—Walking in the Flesh

These patterns will tend to produce the form of faith.

1. Pressure to be perfect; perfectionism as the goal; on-going disappointment with self and others.

2. Self-worth comes from the immediate product that occurs at the beginning of the process; difficulty trusting God. Worry.

3. Reacting; conditional love; impersonal to others except when it serves me; a need to "win"; I'm right, you're wrong; hard heart.

4. Ego-driven, prideful decisions; lack of self-correction; comparison/competition with others, and/or fear of others (they might be more skilled, they might be better at the task); lack of responsibility to admit weakness and/or sin; "secret" choices; personal isolation from community.

God's Perspective—Walking in the Spirit

These patterns will tend to produce faith-based content.

1. Work daily in a purposeful process with the outcome of God's best (His creative design as revealed in Scripture), not my best; achieves an end result with process-based excellence.

2. Self-worth comes from knowing Jesus personally; authentic trust in God; contentment.

3. Responding; unconditional love; personal and sensitive to those around me; non-defensive; openness to truth; confession with a soft heart.

4. Servant-driven; lack of pride base; desire for accountability; lack of comparison and competition; transparency and authentic honesty in the process of learning skills; taking responsibility for weakness and/or sin; no "secret" choices; freedom in Christ to rejoice when others have areas of giftedness I do not possess.

5. Automatic recall from sinful childhood/family patterns (even with awareness, these patterns often appear with an overloaded schedule). Disobedience.

5. Use of supernatural resources provided by the Holy Spirit; choosing self-control (not denial of the problem, passivity, or reacting to others with feelings to overcome sinfull patterns); releasing circumstances to God; healthy schedule choices. Obedience.

6. Not connected to my sinful nature; therefore, I do not tell the truth about "me"; denial of wrongdoing; low self-awareness; no grace for other's mistakes; bad attitudes; lack of forgiveness.

6. Connected and aware of my sin nature; conviction by the Spirit to see myself as I am with choice to operate in grace and love on a daily basis, in all circumstances but especially when I am wronged; able to forgive others; quick to repent.

7. Disrespect of others and exclusion; demanding help from others with a sense of judgment if the help is not given.

7. Respect of others and inclusion; requests help from others with no sense their answer must be yes.

8. No growth in new skill areas because others will see the lack of perfection; legalistic outlook.

8. Growth-oriented risk and change organically (from the inside out).

9. My "rightness" leads me into "sin" choices when I have been sinned against—a sense that if someone treats me wrongly, it's fair game to engage in sinful behavior to that person because of his or her unfairness; slander about the person who treats me wrong is okay if I've been sinned against.

9. My "rightness" leads me to forgive the other party when I have been sinned against. I use the difficult situation as an opportunity to show God's love to the other person; rather than gossip, I choose to pray about and then speak the truth in love to the person gently, considering the possibility that I might be wrong. If I continue to disagree, I do so

with respect and kindness; restoration as the goal of relational interaction.

10. I am a victim in my suffering; Jesus died on the cross to make me "feel better"; the job of the body of Christ is to make me "feel better." Fear-based decisions.

10. I choose by faith to respond to situations that cause me to suffer in a way that pleases God rather than myself. If I suffer, I use the situation as an opportunity to have my character deepened and my obedience to God's ways forged in my soul. I do not see myself as a victim. Courageous decisions.

11. On a practical basis, there is no understanding of biblical submission (to God or to others); desire for power; need to control others. Gossip.

11. Submission to God as well as others who are in leadership unless it violates a higher law of God. Responds to situations with the fruit of the Spirit. Uncomfortable with gossip.

12. "Pat" answers to solve problems; lack of order—chaos.

12. Answers for others reflecting scriptural truth; listens with the heart of Jesus; peace and order.

13. A judgmental, prideful attitude projected to others inferring that all struggles are an indication of spiritual immaturity; inner condemnation from Satan.

13. Humility; freedom in Christ to overcome flesh struggles; thankful for conviction from the Holy Spirit; mercy and compassion for the brokenness in others.

14. Speaking truth to others in the flesh using numbers 1-13 as the emotional environment; reactive anger. Lifestyle decisions leading away from biblical alignment.

14. Speaks the truth to others in love, done gently with no need for ego or power; anger expressed with self-control without reacting for the wrong motives. Deliverance from evil.

"Failing to deal with sin at its root of moral ugliness hinders the flow of God's love and keeps us from experiencing it to the full... When we recognize sin, not just as dangerous but also as deformity, we are prepared to see its remedy (God's love) not just as rescue but as beautiful and satisfying in itself."[35]

---

[35] By John Piper. ©2015 Desiring God Foundation.
Website: desiringGod.org

Walking in the Spirit allows a leader personal freedom in any circumstance. As we look to God for approval, we are free from outside pressures and from others. We don't have to react to leadership challenges in a sinful way. Galatians 1:10 says, "Am I now trying to win the approval of human beings, or of God? Or am I trying to please people? If I were still trying to please people, I would not be a servant of Christ." When Scripture tells us that we will know the truth and that it will set us free (John 8:32), it includes freedom from the approval of others, from our own selfish urges, and from satanic warfare.

Author Toby McKeehan goes even further to articulate why Christ centered leadership works. "When I think of the boldest leaders and thinkers of our world, I believe that Jesus stood above them all. He changed everything, and, by sacrificing His life, He changed the way that I look at my fellowman. He is the one true reason I have a relationship with God. The more I learn about Him, the more I am drawn to Him and His ways. In a world that consists of fake lives and false promises, Jesus is authentic, and He died on the cross to prove it."[36]

The Bottom Line: Passionate Leadership

When dance leadership crucifies sinful motives and exercises spiritual maturity against Satan's schemes, we often walk in the Spirit by answering to God and to others with an obedient heart—soul to sole love. The lack of reaction in the flesh provides the safety, sincere love, healing, and encouragement to continue "the race" (2 Timothy 4:7) in the face of personal challenges, difficult circumstances, and/or relational struggle with others (A true leader becomes the kinesthetic touch of Christ to those around them).

On the other hand, when dance leadership walks in the flesh instead of the Spirit, the sin/challenges that a leader or participant chooses/encounters are not dealt with biblically. Sometimes you become your biggest problem. Isolation in deeply sensitive areas can ruin spiritual growth in the lives of leaders. Carnal choices allow leaders to take refuge

---

[36] Toby McKeehan, *Jesus Freaks: DC Talk and the Voice of Martyrs*, (Tulsa, Oklahoma: Albury Publishing, 1999), 6. Fair use.

in alcohol, shopping, food, pride, insecurity, their own abilities, etc, instead of Jesus. This causes a lack of credibility and witness to the secular world and to others involved in ministry. Be a dance ministry leader who walks in the Spirit rather the flesh. This walk produces both passion and fruit.

"A true and safe leader is likely to be one who has no desire to lead, but is forced into a position by the inward pressure of the Holy Spirit and the press of circumstances. There was hardly a great leader from Paul to the present day but was drafted by the Holy Spirit for the task, and commissioned by the Lord to fill a position he had little heart for.... . The man who is ambitious to lead is disqualified as a leader. The true leader will have no desire to lord it over God's heritage, but will be humble, gentle, self-sacrificing and altogether ready to follow when the Spirit chooses another to lead."[37]

FINAL THOUGHTS ON LEADERSHIP

Soul to Sole Leadership: Personality Test

When I read Personality Plus by Florence Littauer, it opened my eyes to different personality types and leadership styles. Because this was so helpful to me, I encourage you to take the personality test in Appendix C to identify both strengths and weaknesses in your personal leadership style. Use it as a tool for self-awareness and growth.

Once you have completed the personality assessment, consider this:

1. Thank God for the results of the test and celebrate your individual strengths. God doesn't make mistakes; you are a beautiful creature.
2. Don't ignore your weak areas. Weaknesses that are not dealt with will inhibit your leadership. I also believe that God can take weak personality traits and turn them into strengths as you walk in the Spirit.

---

[37] J. Oswald Sanders, *Spiritual Leadership*, (Chicago: Moody Publishers, 1994), 30. Used with permission.

3. Ask God to help you improve in selected areas. The study of the temperaments is to help you understand why you function the way you do.
4. Your personality traits will probably not be concentrated in one category, but you will have more in one area than in the others (The phlegmatic will often find himself spread evenly around).
5. This analysis is for your personal use, but knowledge of the temperaments will help you deal with others.
6. Do not inform people about the personality style that you think they have.
7. Realize that people who are not like you are not wrong; they are just different. But remember, unacknowledged sinful lifestyle choices will inhibit the work of God in your life.

Submission to Pastoral Leadership

In ministry, every good leader must be a follower. Because a choreographer often works with a ministry team that includes directors, worship pastors and tech teams, prayer-in-motion (PIM) leaders must understand biblical submission and how submission leads to unity in a diverse group of people. Understand that a dance leader does not always have the final say on all that occurs in dance ministry. Submission to authority is an unpopular lesson but it's an obedient one. Romans 13:1 says, "Let everyone be subject to the governing authorities, for there is no authority except that which God has established."

Submission means that we are to yield to the will or authority of another. This is a crucial concept to understand as the Christian life is based on submission to Christ. Of course, it is valid to express viewpoints with strong conviction. However, if we are overruled by a higher ministry authority, we need to submit to that decision with the right attitude. Philippians 2:5-11 teaches us, "In your relationships with one another, have the mindset as Christ Jesus: Who, being in very nature God, did not consider equality with God something to be used to his own advantage, rather he made himself nothing, by taking the very nature of a servant, being made in human likeness. And being found in appearance as a man, he humbled himself by becoming obedient to death—even death on a cross! Therefore God exalted him to the highest place and gave him the name that is above every name, that at the name of Jesus every knee should bow, in heaven and on earth and under the earth, and every tongue acknowledge that Jesus Christ is Lord, to the glory of God the Father." It's a challenge to take on the servant attitude of a leader like Jesus, but it's a God-honoring goal for dance ministry; and the Lord Jesus provides us with an incarnate example to follow.

Let's move forward in dance ministry leadership by sharing the gospel visually as we choreograph with the Lord of the Dance. Albert Schweitzer once said, "Example is not the main thing in influencing others, it is the only thing."

Soul to Sole Leadership/Choreography Covenant

Leadership meeting with Pastor Bill Born, Mary Bawden and choreographer Tracey Matney

Now that we've considered the passion to know God, to listen to God, to love God and others, as well as an awareness of the enemy, the differences between walking in the flesh and the Spirit, and the personality evaluation, let's look at the choreography/leadership covenant below (Also, see Appendix D). That is the covenant that you and your pastor will sign before each choreography project begins. May God bless you and your efforts for the kingdom of God!

Leadership/Choreography Covenant

I wish to participate at ____Church/Ministry using my gifts as a leader and/or choreographer, honoring the Lord Jesus through prayer-in-motion. With grace as the foundation, I agree to the following:

a. *All of the conditions listed in the dance ministry member covenant used for the preparation of any prayer-in-motion (See Chapter 5 and Appendix G).*

b. *I want to grow in my personal relationship with Jesus. Because of that, I will spend daily time knowing God, listening to God, and loving God and others. List the personal Bible study you are involved in:_____.*

c. *I commit to be transparent if any disagreements should occur within the context of movement preparation and I commit to speak directly to the person(s) involved. I will use electronic or personal communication with the ministry supervisor regarding any incidents. A decision not to gossip with others will be the philosophical foundation of all interaction.*

d. *I commit to display an attitude of submission to the leaders above me—whether in agreement with those decisions or not—as well as openness to preview input in reference to choreography, music, and costuming choices.*

e. *I commit to the study of the biblical concept being choreographed.*

f. *I resolve to have the integrity to complete any individual project responsibilities agreed upon and to follow through with administrative communication (using a cc format in emails) and completion of the dance/rehearsal process. Active membership at _____ Church.*

g. *I commit to my attendance as leader/choreographer (and attendance of individual choreographers if a program rotates choreographers) at pastoral planning meetings.*

h. *I commit to consistent meetings (as requested) with ____ regarding growth in faith and Bible study, personal interactions with dancers, and the choreography process.*

Date:

Signature of leader:

Name of motion prayer:

Biblical concept targeted for choreography:

Chapter 3

Movement Tools: Motion into the Soul

When I awoke, I smelled smoke and heard odd noises. Outside my house, fire trucks blared warning sirens and people shouted out orders over the alarms. I opened the front door and went outside to see a woman on the phone talking frantically. A fireman told me to move my car down the street if I wanted to leave for work. The house across the street was on fire.

I peered forward, blinking a few times to see if my eyes were playing tricks. The white front door had side windows with blue shutters. It was a welcoming entrance, but there were no other walls to support it. There was nothing left behind the front facade except flames shooting through the charred remains. I watched for a while and wondered why the front wall didn't tip forward and crash.

Then, the fireman hooked up a long hose to the fire hydrant in front of our house. Within minutes, the water began to tame the flames. In the 30-plus years Rich and I had lived in our house, we had never seen that hydrant used. Yet, the right tool at the right time stopped the fire and rescued the land surrounding the neighbor's house. It also rescued our house.

The right tools make a world of difference. That's true for firefighters, mechanics, physicians, and dancers. Certainly, powerful tools coupled with wisdom from Jesus have the potential to equip us for transcendent purposes. And the art of dance, if it is effective, does the same thing. When movement engages the right tools to interact with the heart of Jesus, dance communicates faith in unexpected ways.

"The arts can be extremely powerful. They can awaken us to truth and can change lives."[38]

BACKPACK OF 8 CHOREOGRAPHY TOOLS

Once we understand that dance is a powerful sensory language that moves beyond the intellectual mechanisms that prevent people from listening to God, we can study the craft of choreography so that we can access this non-verbal language. Choreography is a learned skill. If you want to develop a dance ministry, go to classes, workshops, and conferences. Study the books listed in Appendix E.

Beyond on-going enrichment to develop choreography skill, there are eight essential tools to craft movement for prayer-in-motion (PIM) dance ministry. These eight items are what I call the "backpack of tools" to communicate the gospel through dance. An understanding of these skills will equip dancers/choreographers for PIM that "speaks." These tools are:

1. Ongoing, in-depth study of the Scripture to know God, listen to God, and love God and others.

2. Dependence on the Holy Spirit leading the rehearsal and choreography process.

3. Locomotor movement and non-locomotor movement.

4. Movement qualities: percussive, sustained, pendular, collapse, suspend, vibratory, silence.

5. Dance elements: time, space, force, and body.

6. Conceptual technical phrases.

7. Conceptual improvisation: genesis.

8. Observation of participant movement base.

---

[38] Taken from *Heart of the Artist* by Rory Noland. Copyright © 1999 by Zondervan. Use by permission of Zondervan. www.zondervan.com.

Soul to Sole Tools 1 & 2: Ongoing, In-Depth Study of the Scripture to Know God, Listen to God, and Love God and Others with Dependence on the Holy Spirit Leading the Rehearsal and Choreography Process

Chapters 1 and 2 cover the priority of the first two tools for choreography, which also come with a warning.

"In Romans 12:1, the Apostle Paul tells us, offer your bodies as living sacrifices. He goes on to tell us that this is a 'spiritual act of worship.' We need to think about that statement for a minute. Offering our bodies is a spiritual act—it is a physical demonstration of a spiritual reality. Of course, the problem with a living sacrifice is that it keeps trying to crawl off the altar."[39]

Be a living sacrifice that stays on the altar with intentional time to know, listen and love God as you depend on the leading of the Holy Spirit.

Soul to Sole Tool 3: Locomotor and Non-Locomotor Movement

Many choreographers and dancers in the church become overwhelmed as they approach both choreography and/or dance technique for church dance ministry. Most are not professionals and most have a limited dance background. Some have no dance background. With numerous dance styles to draw from (ballet, hip-hop, modern, jazz, tap, etc.) and a plethora of dance techniques to know, it is difficult to decide how to approach movement creation for ministry presentation as well as how to design movement for dancers with a wide range of movement abilities. Moreover, there are a large group of churches nationally who utilize a "worship dance" team on Sunday mornings. These are dancers who give glory to God through movement but have no formal training in the field of dance.

How should we approach dance and choreography in ministry with such a wide range of diversity in age and dance skills? Think with me for a moment. What movement base do all dance forms (including worship dance) have in common?

---

[39] Buddy Owens, *The Way of a Worshiper* (Rancho Santa Margarita, CA: Purpose Driven Publishing, 2005), 69.

The Master Choreographer has the answer. He designed human beings to move in two major ways: locomotor and non-locomotor movement. That technical understanding is the foundation for all formal dance styles, pedestrian movement, and PIM choreography. To understand these terms, let's briefly look at each category and define their meaning.

Locomotor movement is the act or power of moving from place to place (Webster's Dictionary). Locomotor movement "usually involves moving around the wider, available area, with the body not anchored and with complete transfer of weight."[40]

In other words, moving from point A to point B. Basic locomotor movements include walking, jumping, running, hopping, leaping, sliding, galloping, crawling, and skipping. If you analyze the technique base for every dance form, you will see these basic locomotor choices fashioned in a particular technique base with a uniqueness that makes that style stand out. Of course, you can create all kinds of new locomotor movements if you choose. The movements just need to travel from one place to another.

Non-locomotor movement is "movement that moves around the axis of the body (the spine) rather than movement which takes the body through space."[41]

Non-locomotor movement is anchored movement. It stays in one place. Basic non-locomotor movements include bend-straighten, twist-turn, swing-rock, push-pull, curl-stretch, and rise-fall. As with locomotor movement, non-locomotor dance movements are found in every dance technique I have ever seen. They are wonderful choices for choreography creation as well as dancer exploration. Of course, just like locomotor movement, a choreographer can create new non-locomotor movements for any dance.

Is there any dance form or lifestyle movement that does not have locomotor and/or non-locomotor movement as its base? I don't think you can name one. Therefore, because locomotor/non-locomotor movements

---

[40] Phyliss Weikert and Elizabeth B. Carlton, *Foundations in Elementary Education: Movement* (Ypsilanti, MI: High/Scope Press, 1995), 87. Used with permission.

[41] A. Gilbert. (1992) *Creative Dance for All Ages*. Reston, VA: The American Alliance for Health, Physical Education, Recreation and Dance, www.aahperd.org.

cement the foundation for all motion, these two categories are great ways to access choreography for dancers with a variety of abilities. They are also a beginning point for someone who wants to create choreography and doesn't know where to start. By the end of this chapter, you will see how locomotor and non-locomotor design can become a creative way to express movement that goes beyond dance technique.

"The Christian... is free to have imagination. This too is our heritage. The Christian is the one whose imagination should fly beyond the stars."[42]

Soul to Sole Tool 4: Qualities of Movement

As dancers and choreographers, there is more to artistry in movement creation than a technical foundation. Just as you can use your tone of voice to communicate multiple meanings, there are a variety of ways to interpret the same movement with distinctive characteristics. Depending on what you want to convey, you can project a sustained or percussive quality. You may even ask dancers to draw others into the design of a dance with pendular movement or surprise them with a suspension.

Quality: a peculiar and essential character (Webster's Dictionary)

Below are seven movement qualities that assist dancers and choreographers in the movement tools backpack. The condensed definitions below are taken from Modern Dance by Aileen Lockhart.

1. Percussive—sharp. Aggressive movement that is often used for batting, kicking, and striking. Energy is applied with sudden force and then quickly checked.

2. Sustained—extended. Smooth and even movement, which has the result of a steady equalized release of continuous energy. Imagine the way that liquid honey flows from a jar.

---

[42] Taken from *Art & the Bible* by Francis Shaeffer. Copyright (c) 1973 Used by permission of InterVarsity Press, P.O. Box 1400, Downers Grove, IL 60515, USA. www.ivpress.com.

3. Pendular—swinging. Movement that goes to and fro around a fixed center or axis. The energy applied at the beginning of a swing is released as the movement reacts to the pull of gravity.

4. Collapse—give way. Movement that causes a release of tension in a part of the body inducing it to give way. The direction of a collapse is usually downward.

5. Suspend—held until a collapse. A suspension occurs when the pull of two opposing forces is even. The moment of suspension is the brief time when the energy has run out and the moment before the body succumbs to gravity. Suspension can be seen in leaps and in movements using one leg or arm held in the air.

6. Vibratory—shaking. This quality is produced by a quick succession of small percussive movements seen in actions like quivering or shaking.

7. Silence. Movement that stops during a dance.

All of these qualities tend to connect emotions to particular movements. Through the power of the Holy Spirit, they open the heart to respond to faith and add depth to the language of dance.

"The quality of movement is determined by the inherent and essential characteristic or distinctive property that it contains. The particular texture of movement gives it a certain spirit, and by means of contrasting movement qualities shades of expression can be communicated."[43]

Soul to Sole Tool 5: Choreography Elements—Time, Space, Force, and Body

Element: one of the simplest or essential parts or principles of which anything consists, or upon which the constitution or fundamental powers of anything are based (Webster's Dictionary).

"The elements of dance are the meat, the stuff of dancing."[44]

---

[43] Aileene Lockhart, *Modern Dance* (Dubuque, IA: William C. Brown Company Publishers, 1971), 83. Fair use.

[44] Gilbert, 45.

All of the elements chosen for a dance make up its recipe. They capture its unique flavor. However, the knowledge of these elements must be mixed with thorough preparation, allowing dancers and choreographers to move with intentional design. The end result is an audience who gets to taste a dance that is delicious.

So often leaders get ready for ministry situations with a lax attitude. When you get a new choreography project, don't excuse yourself from preparation. Theologian John Stott states my concern much better than I: "'There is no need for me to prepare before preaching [or the choreography],' somebody argues; 'I shall rely on the Holy Spirit to give me the words [or the movement]. Jesus himself promised that it would be given us in that hour what we are to say.' Such talk sounds plausible, until we remember that the misquotation of Scripture is the devil's game. Jesus was referring to the hour of persecution not of proclamation, and to the prisoner's dock in a law court, not the pulpit in a church. Trust in the Holy Spirit is not intended to save us the bother of preparation. The Holy Spirit can indeed give us utterance if we are suddenly called upon to speak and there has been no opportunity to prepare. But he can also clarify and direct our thinking in our study. Indeed, experience suggests that he does a better job there than in the pulpit." [45]

Pray for God's leading and dependence on the Holy Spirit in the rehearsal process. Study the biblical concept and the craft of choreography. Prepare carefully. With that in mind, let's briefly look at the elements for dance composition which have been condensed from Anne Green Gilbert's book, ***Creative Dance for All Ages***, and from a variety of dictionaries:

Time

1. Speed: slow, medium, fast. Every movement you make takes time. We can move many speeds from very fast to very slow.

2. Rhythm: pulse, grouping, pattern, and breath. Rhythm is the pattern of flow or movement. Pulse is an even rhythm. Group puts

---

[45] Taken from *Authentic Christianity* by John Stott, edited by Timothy Dudley-Smith. Copyright (c) 1995. Used by permission of InterVarsity Press, P.O. Box 1400, Downers Grove, IL 60515, USA. www.ivpress.com.

pulses into groups that have different meters. In music, the accent on the first beat of a group helps to identify the meter. Breathing relates to the rhythm of the lungs and is non-metered. Patterns are created by mixing up different beats and accents usually emphasizing a certain beat in a pattern.

Space

1. Place: self and general. The area of space that the body takes up is called self-space or the kinesphere. The rest of the area allowed for movement is general space.

2. Level: low, medium, high. The body can move and create movement from low to high. However, an entire dance needs a variety of levels to enrich what it says through movement.

3. Size (range in relationships): big (far-reach), medium (mid-reach), small (near-reach). Size means how close or how far apart one dancer is to another. How far apart or how close together are three dancers when they dance the same phrase? What do you want the length of their reach to be? Size can also relate to body parts being far and near from the center.

4. Direction: forward, backward, right side, left side, up, down. Use all six directions in choreography creation. Blend several directions in a dance instead of limiting yourself to one direction.

5. Pathway: straight, curved, zigzag. We can create pathways using the body by itself. We can also use pathways on the stage area with straight lines, curved arcs, and a series of lines (zigzag).

6. Focus: single focus, multi-focus. Focus marks the spot where a dancer looks. A dancer can also change focus several times during a dance.

Force

1. Energy: smooth (sustained), sharp (sudden). Energy is the strength and vitality required for sustained activity (Oxford Dictionary). Think of finger-painting for a smooth energy, and think of touching a cactus for sharp energy.

2. Weight: strong, light. Weight refers to a system of units used to express the weight of something (Webster's). If we need a strong degree of force to do an action, muscles show strength. On the other hand, when muscles are relaxed, there is less weight in an action. The more muscles we use, the stronger the force. The fewer muscles we use, the lighter the force.

3. Flow: free, bound. Flow shows how we can move steadily. Free flow movement allows dancers to continually move while the opposite (bound flow) shows limitation or restriction (Oxford).

Body

Body Shapes created to show symmetry

1. Body parts. Dancers need the body and its parts to move in choreography. Sometimes we like to dance with the whole body and sometimes we like to dance with one or two parts.

2. Body shapes: symmetrical, asymmetrical, curved, straight, angular, twisted. The body can become different shapes in PIM creation:

   A. Symmetrical—having similarity in size, shape, and relative position of corresponding parts.

   B. Asymmetrical—irregular in shape or outline.

C. Curved—bent without angles.

D. Straight—successive (without a break).

E. Angular—the space between two intersecting lines or surfaces.

F. Twisted—a thing with a spiral shape; form into a bent, curled, or distorted shape.

3. Relationships. A relationship is a connection between two or more people or things. In dance, we can explore the relationship that our body parts have to one another, the relationship that we have to another dancer, and/or the relationship we have to another object or prop.

4. Balance. Balance is an even distribution of weight ensuring stability. When muscles hold you up and you don't fall, you are on balance. When you are off balance, body weight is no longer over your base of support.

Creating a relationship shape

"You're only kidding yourself if you put creativity before craft."[46]

Whew. We're done listing the elements of dance. I hope you can see why it's important to study them so that you can use them to prepare PIM choreography. The important thing is that your starting point continues to grow. Focus on learning one or two elements during a set amount of time and then intentionally set them into a dance. Don't assume that you know everything you need to know at the beginning of your choreographic journey. On the other hand, don't be discouraged by what you don't know. Just start as God leads and trust Him to help you.

Soul to Sole Tool 6: Biblical Conceptual Technical Phrases

Let's consider the meaning of Biblical Conceptual Technical Phrase so that we can understand how to use these words to create movement.

The word concept indicates an idea, a thought, or a general notion. Furthermore, in choreography for ministry, the word concept actually refers to a biblical concept. From now on when you read the word concept in this book, it refers to a Biblical concept. In the six-step process for choreography in Chapter 4, we will see how the identified biblical concept in a song or text becomes the choreography target for a dance.

Then there is the word technical, which is a derivation of technique. Technique means "relating to a particular craft" (Oxford) and "basic physical movements as used by a dancer" (Webster's). Last, there is the word phrase. A dance phrase is a series of connected movements created by a choreographer for an upcoming ministry dance. What is a "conceptual technical phrase"? A conceptual technical phrase is a series of connected movements created from the dance technique foundation with which you are familiar. These movement choices support the identified concept that you have targeted for choreography. Make sure what you create for a phrase stays within your technical ability.

Let's continue to define and understand the meaning of conceptual technical phrase (also referred to as technical phrase in the rest of this book).

---

[46] Reprinted with the permission of Simon & Schuster, Inc. from *The Creative Habit* by Twyla Tharp with Mark Reiter. Copyright © 2003 W.A.T. Ltd.

1. A conceptual technical phrase is created prior to the start of rehearsals.

2. A conceptual technical phrase is movement that a choreographer creates by using at least one technical dance base (ballet, modern, hop-hop, jazz, worship dance, etc.) for one section of lyrics, text, or music. The series of connected movement steps (dance phrase) are similar to created dance phrases in a studio dance class.

3. Conceptual technical phrases relate and support the conceptual target in the lyrics, text, or music that has been identified (see Chapter 4).

4. There are usually one to five conceptual technical phrases created by a choreographer for every dance.

5. Conceptual technical phrases do not pantomime words. They are not a word-for-word translation of song text.

6. Conceptual technical phrases are completed technical movement steps that a choreographer teaches dancers during the first rehearsal. If the choreographer is led to do so, these steps (identified by dance vocabulary) can be written down on paper so they are ready for the dancers to take home as a handout. These notes will help movers remember what you taught them as they rehearse technical phrases at home. Writing the phrases down will also help the choreographer to prepare for rehearsal.

In choreography, I evaluate the success of what I have created as I watch dancers move through conceptual technical phrases during the first rehearsal. If they don't function as I wish, I must re-work or amend them by the second rehearsal.

Conceptual technical phrases can be complicated or simple. I tend to create more complex technical movement for trained dancers and simpler technical material for untrained or congregational dancers. The reason for this should be obvious. Why would I give technical studio movement to a group of people who have no trained movement base? That would be expecting them to do things they can't do. Never base movement creation on what participants can't do.

If something is too hard technically for participants, I cut it. Whenever I see people looking awkward in movement that is beyond their technical level, they are either under-rehearsed or out of their safety zone, or both. Usually, it is both. There can be no congregational focus on worship or ministry communication when the congregation is "nervous" about the dancers onstage. If the congregation wonders if the dancers can actually do the movement, there is a problem. For the congregation to engage in Spirit-led worship, they can't be focused on any issue other than the worship of Jesus. Keep your priorities straight and design conceptual technical movement based on the realistic assessment of your group.

Below is an example of one technical phrase I prepared for trained dancers in "No More Pain." It was labeled technical phrase #2 when I handed it out to the participating dancers.

Technical Phrase #2:

Walk RL (cts 1, 2) and contract in an improvised "pain" position of your choice (cts 3, 4); walk in a circle to the R (cts 5, 6); step onto L ft as R ft is in a tendu seconde with R arm going in an arc from low R to low L with L hand continuing to circle from low to high (cts 7, 8, 1, 2); stop movement with L hand high above head and L leg in tendu seconde (ct 3); take L arm seconde as L ft lowers (ct 4); side chasse to R as L arm circles (cts 5, 6); step onto R ft with L at parallel passe as L arm cuts through space forward (ct 7); step back onto L ft as R ft stretches fwd (ct 8).

Step into a walking turn to the R with the R, L ft (cts 1, 2); step onto R ft facing wall 5 with L in parallel passe and L arm curved over the head with R curved low to the L (cts 3, 4); step onto L ft with R ft at parallel passe and arms reversing (cts 5, 6); step onto R ft with L ft stretched (cts 7, 8).

Step to corner 2 (ct 1, 2) with the L ft as the R tucks in to lower to the floor ending in a floor turn that ends on knees (cts 3, 4, 5, 6); stand (cts 7, 8). Walk two steps and improvise pain (cts 1-8).

On the other hand, good movement communication can come with simple technical creation. Below is a technical phrase I created for a dance called "I Repent" (popularly sung by Fernando Ortega).[47]

I used three men, who had no background in dance, to portray repentance. This technical phrase ended the dance.

Technical Phrase #1:

And I repent: All three men raise L hand side.

Making no excuses: All three men bend arm into chest with fist clasped.

I repent: All three men slowly look up.

No one else to blame: All three men slowly look down; drop L hand to dangle.

And I return: First man raises arms high.

To fall in love with Jesus: Second man kneels.

I bow down on my knees: Third man kneels.

And I return: First man lowers his arms.

To fall in love with Jesus: Second man lifts head and rises to stand.

I bow down on my knees: Third man lowers hands and looks up.

And I repent: All three men look left in the direction of a cross.

Most of the time, I teach technical phrases slowly during the first rehearsal and then give participants time to work alone for several minutes. During the individual mastery of what I have just taught, I am always available for questions. Next, I go over the technical phrases as the song or accompaniment is played. Then, I give the participating group the option to watch me do the movement up to tempo. I also allow participants to try the technical combinations themselves with the music.

Generally, trained dancers prefer to work with music counts during rehearsal and congregational dancers prefer to use word cues. Interestingly, I have had congregational dancers ask to use music counts during rehearsal while the trained dancers asked to rely on word cues. Do what works.

---

[47] Copyright © 1998 JillyBird Music (ASCAP) Birdwing Music (ASCAP) Meadowgreen Music Company (ASCAP) Devaub Music (ASCAP) Steve Green Music (ASCAP) (admin. at CapitolCMGPublishing.com). All rights reserved. Used by permission.

Soul to Sole Tool 7: Biblical Conceptual Improvisation—Genesis

Improvisation: to make, invent, or arrange on the spur of the moment without planning (Webster's).

The word genesis means "origin or coming into beginning" (Webster's). I use genesis as a synonym for improvisation because when I say improvisation to most participants, it inspires uncertainty and sometimes fear. Don't let that discourage you. If a choreographer has biblical conceptual intent when he or she plans to use genesis, wonderful choreography can be created that gives glory to God and communicates biblical messages. Additionally, genesis activates organic movement that looks natural; and genesis is important because it accesses all levels of technical ability.

Let's condense our understanding of genesis down to the following:

1. Genesis improvisation is a movement plan written by a choreographer. The plan can be long or short.

2. A genesis improvisation engages dancers to create movement spontaneously during rehearsal using the choreographer's written descriptive movement plan.

3. A genesis improvisation plan does not use technical movement terms (i.e. plié, chaine turn, glissade, etc.) from a particular dance style (i.e. ballet, jazz, modern, etc.). Instead, it combines descriptive words that allow for movement choices within the technical range of participants.

4. After the descriptive plan is written, the choreographer distributes it to dancers in a rehearsal on a piece of paper.

5. Dancers read this written movement plan, and they "create" organic movement based on what the descriptive movement plan asks.

6. All genesis improvisations invite dancers to create movement with choices from their own organic base. Like detectives, dancers

"solve" the descriptive movement plan and turn it into actual created movement.

The key for genesis is to have conceptual intent behind the descriptions you want participants to solve. Participants won't have a clue why you are asking for certain kinds of described movements. It's often a good thing they don't know because if they did know, most of them would create boring movements to go with the words. You will be surprised at the invention, the beauty, and the power of what develops if you design genesis with intentional preparation.

There are three conceptual genesis forms to use for PIM: praise poses, phrases, and explorations.

Conceptual genesis praise poses

Praises poses from the early days of SonLight

I use genesis praise poses in almost every dance I choreograph. These are dancer poses that movers create to glorify God. They often portray responsive worship. Praise poses are the easiest tool to design and often the most beautiful visual in a dance. Simply defined, they reflect a body shape done individually or in a group that targets some aspect of the identified concept of a dance.

Conceptual genesis phrases

All genesis improvisations can be written down. However, a genesis phrase has a specific structure that uses the movement words in tools 3-5 from Chapter 3 to initiate conceptual choreography. Once written movement words are chosen, you hand them out, and let the participants make organic movement choices based on the movement descriptions you have requested. Genesis phrases can be conceived based on lyrics, text, and/or counts of music that represent a conceptual choreography target (see Chapter 4, step one).

Below are the movement words to create a written genesis movement phrase for PIM choreography. Of course, every time you write a genesis movement phrase, you don't use all of the words listed below. You use the ones you think will bring out the conceptual intent of the choreography you want in a particular song.

List of descriptive words to use in a genesis movement phrase:

- Tool 3: Locomotor movement, non-locomotor movement.

- Tool 4: Movement qualities: percussive, sustained, pendular, collapse, suspend, vibratory, silence.

- Tool 5: Dance elements:

  Time: speed—slow, medium, fast; rhythm—pulse, breath, pattern, accent.

  Space: place—self and general; level—low, medium, high; size—big, medium, little, near reach, far reach; direction—forward, backward, right side, left side, up, down; pathway—straight, curved, zigzag; focus—single focus, multi focus.

  Force: energy—smooth, sharp; weight—strong, light; flow—free, bound.

  Body: body parts, body shapes—symmetrical, asymmetrical, curved straight, angular, twisted, relationship, balance.

Below is an example of one genesis phrase description that I created for "Redeemer, Savior, Friend" by Darrell Evans and Chris Springer.

Redeemer, Savior, Friend

Use these words to create:

1. Non-locomotor: some kind of high shape with at least one hand stretched out (one or more people). This movement became the word "redeemer" in the lyrics.

2. Non-locomotor: a curl/stretch or twist/turn into a different shape than a high one; it should change level. This movement became the word "Savior" in the lyrics.

3. Non-locomotor: a three person connected shape: two people touching personally; one person connected to the shape taking weight. This movement became the word "friend" in the lyrics.

When you hand out the written genesis phrase in the first rehearsal, make sure that you don't include the song lyrics or text (if your choreography project is a song with words or uses a text) that go with each line of written description.

Genesis phrase for eight lines of lyrics in "Take Heart, My Friend"[48] by Juan Fernando Ortega and John Andrew Scheiner (This phrase was longer than most).

Create:

1. Two locomotor steps for both dancers; non-locomotor connected shape with pendular action ending with one dancer higher than the other.

2. Non-locomotor: A) One dancer changes direction to connect with the other dancer; both dancers have different levels. B) One dancer jumps to become upright with asymmetrical shape. C) Two person suspension that ends in a collapse; one dancer circles the arm while the other dancer stands.

---

[48] "Take Heart, My Friend" by John Andrew Schreiner & Fernando Ortega © 2004 John Andrew Schreiner Music (admin. by Lori Kelly Rights & Licenses) & Cerdo Verde Music (admin. by Curb Songs) / Curb Songs / John Andrew Schriener Music. All Rights Reserved. Used By Permission.

3. Four forward locomotor shapes done one by one with dancers connecting: one-by-one focus is anywhere but at the audience.

4. Non-locomotor: connected symmetrical movement (with two level changes) that is sustained and ends facing side.

5. Non-locomotor: two intimate kinds of touch; each dancer should change direction; then a locomotor turn for both dancers.

6. Non-locomotor: two different percussive movements done at the same time; locomotor, weighted body shape where one dancer carries or drags the other; it ends with dancers looking up.

7. Toe-to-toe locomotor walk (in directed syncopation) to walls 6 and 8 in opposite directions with the head down; dancer one forms a conceptual praise pose; dancer two runs in a curve and enters dancer one's conceptual praise pose.

8. Same symmetrical arm movement that is done as a duo on a low body level, on a medium body level, and on a high body level; dancers need to face different directions as they do the same movements.

Now think through the words from the song that match the genesis phrase description for this section of the dance. Note that each line of genesis was created for each line of the song.

1. *If we should falter when trouble surrounds us.*

2. *When the wind and the waves are wild and high.*

3. *We will look away to Him who rules the waters.*

4. *Who spoke His peace to the angry tide.*

5. *He is our Comfort, our Sustainer.*

6. *He is our help in time of need.*

7. *And when we wander He is our Shepherd.*

8. *He who watches over us never sleeps.*

Let's look at four other examples of a genesis phrase. Note that examples one and two indicate specific counts for the genesis phrase while examples three and four do not. It's up to you to decide.

Example One—Create:

1. Non-locomotor movement using sustained arm movement quality (cts 1-4).

2. Two locomotor movements (cts 5-8).

3. Non-locomotor praise shape (cts 1-4).

4. Hold non-locomotor praise shape and circle the hands (cts 5-8) with a level change.

Example Two—Create:

1. Non-locomotor shape with percussive movement quality (cts 1-8).

2. Non-locomotor movement with sustained movement quality (cts 1-8).

3. Non-locomotor movement that changes to two different body parts (cts 1-4).

4. Locomotor movement done in a curved pathway (8 cts).

Example Three—Create in 2s:

1. Non-locomotor: one sustained movement that finishes at an angle.

2. Non-locomotor: one symmetrical movement that has a percussive movement quality.

3. Locomotor: either one repeated L movement or several different locomotor movements that take dancers from point A to point B in a straight pathway.

4. Non-locomotor: a pendular movement that changes into a high praise pose.

5. Non-locomotor: one medium shape that goes to a low shape with two changes of direction.

Example Four

1. Non-locomotor: create a group praise shape with all three levels: low, medium, and high.

2. Locomotor: using a sustained quality, slowly release from the group shape to stand full front one by one; the last person walks somewhere away from the line of dancers that has formed.

3. In groups of two, create a twisted, asymmetrical shape; turn that shape into a symmetrical shape.

4. Locomotor: two dancers leave their duo and walk to another duo to join them; create a non-locomotor suspended shape.

5. Non-locomotor: release the suspension and circle the right hand in whatever direction you find yourself. One dancer kneels as he or she circles the R hand.

The worksheet in Appendix F provides all the descriptive movements and direction for genesis and technical phrase creation and guidance thus far discussed in this chapter. This handy, at-a-glance tool will help you to utilize and organize genesis dance creation.

Genesis Phrase Creation Tips:

*   Write one line of genesis phrase description for one to two lines of song lyrics.

*   Begin each section of the written movement phrase by specifying whether you want locomotor or non-locomotor movement. Then specify a quality of movement for your movement design (if you want one). This helps clarify your intention to the dancers.

*   Add other movement words as you are led but be clear in what you ask for. Your descriptions are not limited to the list in this chapter and the same ones listed in Appendix F.

*   Record the created movement that is developed in a genesis rehearsal on digital video. Go home, mute any sounds in the rehearsal recording, and play the section of the music, words, or Bible text that you had in mind when you wrote a descriptive

phrase for genesis creation. You will be able to see and hear if the two components work together. Often, I find myself cutting part of the participant material to use within the choreography for a dance. When you describe a genesis phrase, it's best to have too much material rather than too little.

- Remind dancers to relax and enjoy the process no matter the final dance product.

- Encourage dancers to avoid judging their movement choices. They should understand that their task is to follow the movement descriptions and "solve" each description. Genesis should be fun once dancers trust you and the process.

Conceptual genesis explorations

The third genesis movement option to use in Soul to Sole Choreography involves conceptual explorations. Using the genesis exploration method, I create improvisations targeting the identified conceptual intent that I want to sketch in movement communication. The description does not use the same kinds of movement words as a genesis phrase. Generally, genesis explorations take deeper abstract thinking beyond the skill of a descriptive genesis phrase or a genesis praise pose. It might be best to create genesis explorations after you have choreographed for a while.

In "Jesus, I Am Resting, Resting" (by Jean S. Pigott, 1876), you will see prayer-in-motion developed from the genesis explorations listed below. Numbers 1 and 2 describe what I asked the dancers to do from a first-person perspective. Numbers 3 and 4 use the exact wording I handed out to dancers for genesis exploration at the time that this dance was created.

1. I demonstrated examples of back-to-back movement, suspensions, pulls, and weight shapes. Then I asked the group to divide into twos so that they could create back-to-back movement, suspensions, pulls, and weight shapes for themselves; next, I asked them to create a sequence with their partner demonstrating three of the four elements that they were shown.

2. After I defined 'rest in the Lord,' I asked participants to tell me a personal story of spiritual rest and I provided them with pen and paper to write their 'rest' story using three sentences (describe a problem you had; describe how 'rest' was not occurring; and describe how God helped you rest in the situation). Finally, I asked participants to create a frozen shape for each sentence of the story with the following structure:

   a. Involve the hands to tell the first part of the story.

   b. Express the situation that needed rest with the whole body.

   c. Show how God ministered to you and gave you rest using a change of direction and level. Combine the frozen shapes of individual people into a duet to form a dance phrase.

3. Divide into two large groups. Have one group create a way to move across the stage showing "rest"; have the other group create a weighted shape of their choice (demonstrating "rest").

4. In twos, use contact movement initiated from finger to finger (or hand to hand) involving two other parts of the body (i.e. head, shoulders) to create a sequence.

5. Here are two additional ideas for simple genesis explorations:

   a. Choose a noun: describe that word using adjectives; take the adjectives and choose a movement shape for each adjective. Then string the movements together to form a phrase.

   b. Triangle improvisation: three people form a triangle formation; one person leads the other two in slow movement that they can easily copy with the leader is the top of the triangle. The leadership changes at a given time with the second person as the leader, and then later, the third.

Use genesis creation in your choreography—praise poses, phrases, and explorations. Remember that genesis is structured improvisation.

Always give participants the option to participate in genesis choices. Voluntary participation invites them into safe movement design. Always encourage, encourage, encourage. Genesis will access organic communication from dancers of all levels and break up similar movements that choreographers tend to create for each dance.

Men excel using the genesis method. I used genesis phrase creation almost exclusively in "Redeemer, Savior, Friend" because I had three untrained men in that dance and their movement choices allowed them to look relaxed in front of a secular audience. The dance won finalist status in a nationally known choreography festival.

Don't underuse this tool! It will open up your choreography tool base and glorify God in movement creation!

One section of a genesis phrase using men with no movement background; 'Redeemer, Savior, Friend' won finalist status for the 2002 National Choreography Festival in Palm Springs

"Without knowledge, one's movement responses cannot develop and grow . . . . skills must be developed, in relation to the concepts. The development of skills will improve the compositions and increase the level of creativity."[49]

---

[49] Gilbert, 4.

Soul to Sole Tool 8: Observation of Participant Movement Base

This last tool sounds superfluous. It isn't. In PIM, there is incredible diversity in the dance technique of participants. I often observe dancers as they rehearse and then modify choreography to suit their technical ability. Since there is a vast array of movement choices in choreography, simplify your technical phrase creation so that participants can easily do what you choreograph. Utilize genesis. That way a congregation can focus on the Spirit-led worship of Jesus.

As you reflect on your backpack of resources for PIM presentation, remember that dance is its own language. Learn how to speak the language by activating these eight tools:

1. Ongoing, in-depth study of the Scripture to know God, listen to God, and love God and others.

2. Dependence on the Holy Spirit leading the rehearsal and choreography process.

3. Locomotor movement and non-locomotor movement.

4. Movement qualities: percussive, sustained, pendular, collapse, suspend, vibratory, silence.

5. Dance elements: time, space, force, and body.

6. Conceptual technical phrases.

7. Conceptual improvisation: genesis.

8. Observation of participant movement base.

WARNING: NO EROTIC MOVEMENT

Create technical conceptual phrases from a technical movement base coupled with the study of the identified choreography target. Use genesis as a foundation for organic movement design based on the same conceptual target. However, be aware that there is a warning for the creation of either technical or genesis choreography: limitations in movement choices. Most secular artists do not tolerate limits in movement choices. The restrictions come when PIM choreography uses erotic movements.

Erotic means tending to arouse sexual excitement (Oxford). Erotic movement nullifies the worship of Jesus and the communication of biblical truth. Chapter 5 will discuss why it is important to have a group of committed Christians preview a dance before it is presented. The good news is that there are plenty of movements to choose from that will stretch the boundaries of movement language with purposeful and godly design.

Remember:

1. Pray and trust God to guide you by His Spirit.

2. Identify the worship category and the targeted concept of a dance. Mentally re-visit the biblical concept over and over again as you design choreography.

3. Prepare and commit to what you do. Don't be afraid.

4. Pray, study, and prepare.

   "Dance was created to be a functioning, powerful tool of communication in the Kingdom of God to his glory."[50]

---

[50] Ann Stevenson, *Restoring the Dance* (Shippensburg, PA: Destiny Image Publishers, 1998), 21.

Chapter 4

Soul to Sole Choreography:
Six Steps to Prayer-in-Motion

"Your word is a lamp for my feet, a light on my path" (Psalm 119:105).

"Jesus is God in human, bodily form. Jesus used bodily movement in this world as a way of revealing his true personhood, both before and after his crucifixion. Dance can bring all this back to us, reminding us that he himself lived an authentic human existence."[51]

Jesus moved as Lord of the dance; He mastered prayer-in-motion (PIM). As a man, Jesus came to demonstrate worship and to model God's love through praise, beauty, teaching, celebration, and prayer. When a choreographer understands which of these categories a dance represents and then further clarifies the intent of created movement with a specific conceptual choreography target, he or she transforms soul movement into sole movement. The result is PIM choreography that connects the heart to activated faith.

CONCEPTUAL CHOREOGRAPHY FOR PRAYER-IN-MOTION

Yes, movement tools are necessary for good choreography. They are crucial elements that aid PIM movement design. But, by themselves, these tools are not ministry. Ministry is targeted choreography communicating a biblical concept that dances into the soul. Without Holy Spirit directed intentionality, it is easy for a dance to say nothing. Robert

---

[51] Savage, 64.

Webber said it clearly: "When dance is initiated in worship, it is often used to express the healing presence of God."[52]

In Chapters 1 and 3, I wrote about the meaning of "concept." We discovered Webster's Dictionary defines a concept as an idea, a thought, a general notion. Then we learned that PIM choreography identifies biblical concepts. In other words, PIM reveals choreography based on the principles found in Scripture.

Similarly, the Oxford English Dictionary, defines principle as a fundamental truth serving as the foundation for belief or action. In this book, I identify a biblical principle as a synonym for a biblical concept. These principles lead a Christian to understand the heart of God and to do what pleases Him (Proverbs 3:5-7).

A biblical concept works with endless variables. For instance, consider the concept of love. The Bible defines agape love as an attribute of God and as a Christian virtue. But the variables (or the specific ways) to live out God's love are endless. In other words, there is not one correct way to show the concept of love. I might love my husband by cooking him dinner while you might love a homeless person by helping at a homeless shelter. Another person might choose to forgive an enemy. But these examples are all ways to live out the concept of love.

The same understanding applies to choreography with biblical conceptual intent. To design motion with conceptual intent, you must clearly understand the general idea, thought, or notion of a biblical concept. If you do, you can plug in an endless array of genesis and technical dance movement to support the concept in the language of dance. Therefore, you can choreograph biblical concepts because specific movements and different tools are variables. It will be your understanding of conceptual intent that will be the critical component in successful ministry creation.

Now for an important clarification: Creating choreography is different than accessing technical movements. Although movement creation is a learned craft, you can be a gifted and called dancer who is not cut out to create choreography, and you can be a gifted and called choreographer

---

[52] Taken from *Discipleship Journal*, "From Jerusalem to Willow Creek" by Robert Webber. Copyright © 1992,

12, no. 70. Used by permission of Tyndale House Publishers, Inc. All rights reserved.

without having strong technical dance skill. The two areas do not necessarily overlap. Listen to God and let others affirm both the call and the gifting in one or both of these areas. Be aware that you may enjoy movement and not have a call or a gifting for dance ministry in either area.

We have already said that choreography is a learned craft. With a call and a gifting, you will improve and get better in your movement communication. Remember to study, prepare, and pray before rehearsals begin. Watch out for pride and fear. Both qualities can warp your soul and diminish skill development. If you operate in pride, you won't acknowledge failure, insecurity, or weakness (Proverbs 16:18). On the other hand, if you operate in fear, you won't have the strength to move forward in the choreography and leadership process (Romans 8:15). Much of the time, Satan attacks us in both areas (1 Peter 5:8). Confess both fear and pride. Then use God's call and gifting in dance to move forward in the choreography process.

Honest personal evaluation purifies prayer-in-motion design. A clean soul honors God's leading and stops pride or fear from diverting you onto a "rabbit trail." In PIM choreography, a "rabbit trail" takes you off the intended conceptual target of the dance that you are preparing. It is a warning. Remember to point your conceptual design back to God using prayer, study, and preparation.

Before we study the six steps of how to choreograph prayer-in-motion, let's review the movement tools. These resources provide worshipful choices for each step of Soul to Sole Choreography:

1. Ongoing, in-depth study of the Scripture to know God, listen to God, and love God and others.

2. Dependence on the Holy Spirit leading the rehearsal and choreography process.

3. Locomotor movement and non-locomotor movement.

4. Movement qualities: percussive, sustained, pendular, collapse, suspend, vibratory, silence.

5. Dance elements: time, space, force, and body.

6. Conceptual technical phrases.

7. Conceptual improvisation: genesis.

8. Observation of participant movement base.

SIX STEPS TO SOUL TO SOLE CHOREOGRAPHY

"In order to be creative, you have to know how to prepare to be creative."[53]

1. Identify a biblical concept in the song or text using an inductive analysis of the words. Study the concept so that you have a deeper understanding of it. Then decide on the worship category or categories for the choreography.

2. Choose three or four repeated phrases or words from the song or written text that highlight the biblical concept.

3. Choreograph dance movement to these song or text lyrics using one of the following techniques:

   A. Conceptual technical phrases that you choreograph prior to the beginning of rehearsal.

   B. Genesis structured improvisation that you describe prior to rehearsal using conceptual praise poses, conceptual phrases, and/or conceptual explorations.

4. Prepare a written handout for the dancers that includes the movement score: song lyrics, inductive analysis, technical phrases and genesis movement, time signature, choreography target, worship category, biblical research, and a rough outline of where you plan to put your technical phrases and genesis movement.

5. Using the choreography tools listed in Chapter 3, continue to design movement for the third and fourth rehearsals to paint a biblical conceptual picture.

---

[53] Tharp, 9.

6. Leave 10-20 percent of the dance choreographically open so that the Holy Spirit can continue to lead the direction of the choreography as you work within the technical level of the participants.

Soul to Sole Step 1

Soul to Sole Step 1: Identify a biblical concept in the song or text choice using an inductive analysis of the words. Study the concept so that you have a deeper understanding of it. This biblical concept will serve as the choreography target for the message that you want to communicate for dance ministry in the language of dance. Then decide on the worship category or categories for the choreography.

To start this investigation, let me clearly define what I mean by inductive. This word simply means to reason "from particular facts to a general conclusion." In other words, the choreographer does not decide what the message of a song or text is. You find this out logically by observing it for repeated words along with descriptive details. At the end of this inductive analysis, the repeated word(s) in the song or text will identify the biblical concept to choreograph (By the way, the examples for inductive analysis used in this chapter are all songs).

Inductive investigation rarely goes wrong unless the song or text has no content. When that happens, there tends to be few repeated words/phrases. Occasionally, a song describes an attribute of God or a specific biblical concept, and does not repeat phrases or words. But this is rare. Normally, repeated words and phrases make conceptual identification easy. After that initial analysis, look at the worship categories (praise, beauty, teaching, celebration, and prayer) and decide which one(s) best fit the chosen song or text. The next step is to observe other song details. The Holy Spirit will use these observations to guide your choreography creation. Does the song highlight images and comparisons? If so, list them. Does the text compare themes that target good versus evil, or does it focus on humanity's ways versus God's ways? Does the content use adjectives in unique ways that paint clear meaning? What does the song say about the person or character of God? What do the words teach about right and wrong? What do the lyrics teach about relationships, friendships, and marriage? Is the song more about us than God? Is there a realistic portrayal of emotions? Finally, how are false belief systems portrayed? Don't look for the same answers in each song. Each project will have a different outcome.

Of course, you should also observe the musical structure of the song. By that, I mean that you will need to notice where the verses, chorus repeats, and transitional interludes occur. At the same time, you will also need to determine the time signature in a song, usually 4/4 or 3/4. If you are not sure how to do this, ask a musician for help. In time, you will begin to hear the meter on your own.

Often, I create movement phrases to go with a set time signature. Other times I make the movement fit a certain meter. But I always observe the meter of the song before I start choreography. At this beginning stage, concept identification, worship category, text observation, and time signature will all impact movement design and the eventual goal of movement communication. Below is an inductive analysis of a song called "Jesus, I Am Resting, Resting" (by Jean S. Pigott, 1876). Note that when I do an inductive analysis of a song, I use colored pencils to indicate repeated words, phrases and observations. In the analysis below, I use the computer tools of bold, italics and underlining to do the same thing.

Jesus, I Am Resting, Resting

CHORUS 1:
Jesus I am <u>resting, resting</u>
In the joy of what thou art
I am finding out the greatness
Of thy *loving* heart

Verse 1:
Thou hast bid me gaze upon me
And thy beauty fills my soul
For by thy transforming power
Thou hast made me whole

CHORUS 2:
Jesus I am <u>resting, resting</u>

In the joy of what thou art
I am finding out the greatness
Of thy *loving* heart

Verse 2:
Simply trusting thee Lord Jesus
I behold thee as thou art
And thy *love* so pure so changeless
Satisfies my heart
Satisfies my deepest longings
Meets, supplies its every need
Compasseth me round with blessings
Thine is *love* indeed.

CHORUS 3:
Jesus I am <u>resting</u>, <u>resting</u>
In the joy of what thou art
I am finding out the greatness
Of thy *loving* heart

Verse 3:
Ever lift thy face upon me
As I work and wait for thee.
Resting 'neath thy smile Lord Jesus
Earth's dark shadows flee
Brightness of my Father's glory
Sunshine of my Father's face
Keep me ever trusting, **resting**
Fill me with thy grace.

CHORUS 4:
Jesus I am <u>resting</u>, <u>resting</u>
In the joy of what thou art
I am finding out the greatness
Of thy *loving* heart

CHORUS 5:
Jesus I am <u>resting</u>, <u>resting</u>
In the joy of what thou art

I am finding out the greatness
Of thy *loving* heart
I am finding out the greatness
Of thy *loving* heart

Inductive Analysis (referring to the lyrics above):

Chorus is repeated 5x—note that the chorus is bolded.

Note that the phrases "I am finding out the greatness" and "of thy loving heart" are repeated 6x (1x more than the other lines of the chorus repeats; because of this, these two lines have a different font).

"Resting" is repeated 11x—note this word is underlined.

"Love/loving" is repeated 8x—note that forms of this word are in italics.

Observe the first person description of rest, which each verse describes personally.

Verbs that show the activation of faith are trusting, satisfies, meets, supplies, compasseth, finding, resting, work, wait, fill.

Identify the word or phrase in the lyrics that is repeated the most number of times. That will usually identify the choreography target for the song. In these lyrics, "Jesus, I Am Resting, Resting" is repeated 5x and the individual word resting is repeated 11x. Both the repeated phrase and the word demonstrate the strongest message in this song because we see them in the lyrics again and again.

Often the biblical concept in a song appears in the title. The song title "Jesus, I Am Resting, Resting" reflects the identified target discovered in our inductive analysis. But as an investigator in the identification stage, don't think that you can always go with the title to reveal the message of the song. There are instances that title and content don't match. However, in this conceptual identification stage, we don't assume or guess what the target is. We know what the target is because the repeated words in the text that we see most frequently reveal the biblical concept. Before we leave our discussion of "Jesus, I Am Resting, Resting," let's identify the worship category to help frame the choreography correctly. The categories for this song are praise and beauty (healing).

Now let's analyze the words for another dance. The title is "No More Pain" by Geoff Thurman, Becky Thurman, and Michael English.[54]

"No More Pain"

Verse 1:
She sits by the window
With wandering eyes
She has a song in her heart
And a golden disguise;
Her body is torn
Because age doesn't heal
She's not letting on
About the *PAIN* that she feels
But she knows in her soul
That it won't be too long
Till Jesus comes back to carry her home
Where there will be

CHORUS 1:
*No more **PAIN**, **no more sorrow**, **no more** waiting for illusive tomorrows,*
*There will be **no more PAIN**, **no more dying**, **no more** striving or strain—*
No more PAIN

Verse 2:

---

[54] Michael English/Becky Thurman/Geoffrey Thurman, © 1993 Dayspring Music, LLC, P.E. Velvet Music, Seventh Son Music, Inc. All rights reserved. Words and music by Geoff Thurman, Becky Thurman and Michael English. Copyright ©1993 Seventh Son Music, Inc., P.E. Velvet Music (a div. of Harding Music Group) (ASCAP) and Dayspring Music, LLC. All rights for Seventh Son Music, Inc. Administered by BMG Rights Management (US) LLC. All rights reserved. Used by permission. *Reprinted by permission of Hal Leonard Corporation.* (Adm. By Carol Vincent and Associates, LLC.)

My mind's eye remembers
The trouble I've seen
All I have been through
And how I long to be free
But I learn by her patience
That I need her resolve
To wait for the opening
Of Eternity's halls
And I know that in time
We will stand side by side
When Jesus comes back receiving his bride

CHORUS 2:

There will be **no more PAIN**, **no more sorrow**, **no more** *waiting for illusive tomorrows,*
There will be **no more PAIN**, **no more dying**, **no more** *striving or strain—*
No more PAIN

CHORUS 3:

No more PAIN **no more sorrow**, **no more** *waiting for illusive tomorrows*
There will be **no more PAIN**, **no more dying**, **no more** *striving or strain*

CHORUS 4:

No more
No more PAIN, **no more sorrow**, **no more** *waiting for illusive tomorrows*
No more PAIN, **no more dying**, **no more** *striving or strain*
No more PAIN
No more PAIN

Inductive Analysis of "No More Pain" (referring to the lyrics above):
In "No More Pain," we underlined the title of the song 12 times. Furthermore, four repeated choruses include two words that are similar to pain which are sorrow and dying. Last, pain is personified in the musical

arrangement. Did you notice that the story is told from the third person and first person perspective? A third person perspective narrates a story with description while the first person perspective tells it personally. All of these observations identify the choreography target of "No More Pain." The identified biblical concept of this song is "No More Pain."

Your inductive analysis notes could look like this:

- "No more pain" is repeated 12x.

- "No More" is repeated 29x.

- Chorus is repeated 4x; the chorus includes two synonyms (words that have a similar meaning)—sorrow and dying—for the word pain; all three words are in a bold font while pain is also underlined. The use of these three words makes the message of the song even stronger.

- Pain is personified in the musical arrangement.

- The story is told from a first and third person perspective. Words like I or my refer to a first person perspective; words like she and her refer to the third person.

- "Pain" is repeated 13x; "sorrow" and "dying" are repeated 8x.

Although the song's message contains the hope of heaven, the song style itself communicates great personal pain. The challenge of the choreography was to develop all sides of the concept: the hope of heaven versus pain, sorrow, and dying. Notice that the biblical concepts presented in this song are in fact biblical because we can find these concepts in Scripture. In Revelation 21:4, the pain aspect is featured: "He [God] will wipe every tear from their eyes. There will be no more death or mourning or crying or pain, for the old order of things has passed away." In John 16:33, the hope aspect is featured: "In this world you will have trouble. But take heart! I have overcome the world."

"No More Pain" represents clear biblical teaching. However, if I hadn't evaluated this song inductively, I would have missed the richness of the hope that ran alongside its expressed pain. For this reason, in the choreography that God gave me, I added the figure of Jesus walking through the pain of the dancers to equip them with peace. The visual wouldn't be meaningful without hope. Remember not to overlook text observation. Now let's think through the five categories of worship for identification in "No More Pain." The song emphasizes teaching and beauty (healing).

Group Shot of 'No More Pain' at the 2003 National Choreography Festival In Palm Springs, CA including lighting designer Diane Kuehl (in vest) , drama participant Jan Arnwine (in black dress) and Anaiah Simons (child). The drama in 'No More Pain' was incorporated into the dance prior to presentation.

Rabbit trail warning 1

Leave the results of conceptual investigation to the word analysis of the song. Don't assume that you know it.

Rabbit trail warning 2

It is easy to ignore the concept in a song and focus on feelings or technique as you plan choreography to the music. Neither feelings nor technique should lead the craft of planned choreography. Feelings are engaged as you respond to Jesus in worship. Technique will be used to prepare the dance but neither one are the foundation of movement design.

If you are responding to the worship of Jesus spontaneously in a church service, that is biblical and valid. However, that kind of responsive movement reflects a different dance form than planned and rehearsed choreography. This six-step Soul to Sole Choreography method detailed here is planned dance ministry as led by the Holy Spirit (Planned movement must be Spirit-led every bit as much as spontaneous movement). Moving onstage without intent will not translate clearly to those who watch you move. Typically, the congregation will not understand what you are doing, and the pastoral staff will not embrace dance ministry.

Once the concept and worship category have been identified, you, as choreographer, must find a way to develop them in your choreography. Otherwise, you're wasting the non-verbal language of dance. After all, why dance to a song about "rest" or "no more pain" and not show movement that enhances its meaning? If you decide that you don't want to do the concept of rest or pain, you can set the song aside and look at the words to a different song. But the message of the song mustn't be ignored.

Rabbit trail warning 3

Don't assume that a Christian song will have a rich source of theology. Christian composers often follow rabbit trails. It is easy to like a song because of its arrangement (the beat, the meter, the style of the singer, etc.) rather than song content. If a song has no biblical content, toss it. Although a song can dabble in Christian themes, it is not a good choice for dance ministry if the message is not clear.

Rabbit trail warning 4

Don't choreograph a song that you can't understand even if the song includes a clear biblical message after inductive analysis. The weak singing and musical arrangement overrides its content. Why? Because a congregation has one time to see a dance, hear the words, and walk away with a message. If they can't understand the words of a song, their focus shifts from learning about God to straining to hear the words of the song.

Rabbit trail warning 5

Consider the artistic style of the song. With inductive analysis, you have already noted the words in the music. This assumes that a particular song has passed choreographic evaluation with flying colors. Now take the song style and music arrangement into consideration. How do you decide on the number of people to participate in a particular dance project? This conclusion should focus on what's best for communicating the biblical message and not merely on personal whim.

God will help you in this process as choreographic choices blend with the creative style of the music. A solo or a duet of dancers is a choice best served with songs that are sung as solos, or that project quiet reflection. Two to five voices in the song background will lend themselves to a small group of dancers numbering from three to eight. When a song has multi-voices in it, dance choreography should reflect that power with a multitude of dancers onstage. Be careful. Don't weaken your choreography by making movement decisions that will not fulfill the energy or the quietness of the music.

Rabbit trail warning 6

Ask yourself what genders and ages will best express the identified message of the song. Generally, God designed men to express power and strength while women tend to reflect softness and beauty. Children are often wonderful communicators as well. Sometimes a project needs only men, and sometimes a project needs only women. On the other hand, many dances are best communicated with the involvement of both genders and ages. Those decisions must be based on the message of choreography, the singers in the song, and the arrangement of the music.

Rabbit trail warning 7

Study the identified concept in the song. Don't focus solely on movement. Get out your Bible and dig deep into Scripture. This will impact the movement that you create. Use other books to amplify your knowledge. Another nifty resource is the Internet. Below are several websites that can broaden your understanding of whatever identified concept you are looking for:

crosswalk.com
biblegateway.com
wordsearchbible.com
pcstudybible.com

Fill your mind with definitive teaching and Scripture about the targeted concept for choreography. Meditate on one Scripture as you make movement choices. God will use it to renew your mind and show His glory. You can also share the highlights from your research with the dancers as you rehearse. With the Holy Spirit as your primary Teacher, look to God to embody prayer-in-motion in you so that choreographed prayer-in-motion embodies Him. Watch God grow you and the dancers when you truly understand His heart.

Soul to Sole Step 2

Soul to Sole Step 2: Choose three or four repeated phrases or words from the song or written text that highlight the biblical concept.

Let's list the repeated phrases and words from the song examples that I used in step 1 in order to understand step 2:

A) Repeated words and phrases from "Jesus, I Am Resting, Resting"

- "Jesus, I Am Resting, Resting," (chorus repeated 5x) *Jesus I am resting, resting, in the joy of what thou art, I am finding out the greatness, of thy loving heart.*

- Loving/love (repeated 8x)

- Resting (repeated 11x)

B) Repeated words and phrases from "No More Pain"

- "No More Pain," (chorus repeated 4x). *No more pain, no more sorrow, no more waiting for illusive tomorrows, there will be no more pain, no more dying, no more Striving or strain–no more pain*

- No more pain (repeated 12x)

- Pain (repeated 13x with sorrow and dying 8x)

- No more (repeated 29x)

In this stage of the choreographic process, we have not yet designed any movement. Don't get ahead of yourself. Take your time. If you have done the inductive analysis correctly, this step will be over sooner than you can blink (er, think). These identified words and phrases are where choreography creation starts. After that, move to step 3 of the Soul to Sole Choreography process.

Soul to Sole Step 3

Soul to Sole Step 3: Choreograph dance movement to these song or text lyrics using one of the following techniques:

- *Conceptual technical phrases that you choreograph prior to the beginning of rehearsal.*

- *Genesis movement that you describe prior to rehearsal using conceptual praise poses, conceptual phrases, and/or conceptual explorations.*

In Chapter 3, you learned that a conceptual technical phrase was a movement phrase created by the choreographer prior to the start of a rehearsal using a specific technical base. Chapter 3 also said that technical phrases should be written after you have created them so they are ready for the dancers to take home at the end of the first rehearsal. Technical dance phrases use technical dance words like plie, tendu, etc.

Remember that conceptual genesis movement is a written descriptive movement plan created by a choreographer. I particularly recommend for you to use praise poses and genesis phrases in your choreography creation. If you create genesis phrases, note that genesis phrases develop from movement tools 3-5 (locomotor and non-locomotor movement, movement qualities and dance elements). Also be aware that technical phrases, like genesis phrases, are subjective. There is not one right way to create either a technical phrase or a genesis phrase. The choice of movement depends on variables that come from the identified concept. Generally, positive conceptual themes like grace, love, mercy, forgiveness, etc. must have an open, hopeful quality to them while opposite themes often use contraction and/or weighted movement to represent sin or lack of forgiveness.

Extract movement from people based on what they can do. Dancers will look confident and worshipful if they are asked to move inside their "safety zone." A safety zone is the movement area that participants can access with low stress.

As choreographer, you make the choice as to what kind of movement—technical or genesis—that you wish to create for a ministry project. In either case, you need to take responsibility for this important part of dance creation. Don't hesitate to initiate choreography with technical phrases or genesis movement in step three because it won't appear by itself. Pray for God to help you (See Appendix F for the form to create genesis/technical phrase movement).

Rabbit trail warning 8

Prepare carefully for the first rehearsal. It's a waste of your time and participants' time if you don't come to the first rehearsal with a completed inductive analysis of the song or text and a structural way to label what you hope to do. If you're not up to this kind of preparation, perhaps choreography is not your call. Obviously, you, along with the group, will pray for the Holy Spirit's guidance, but don't use that as an excuse not to be ready for the first rehearsal.

Rabbit trail warning 9

Craft genesis praise poses, genesis phrases, and genesis explorations carefully and clearly. Your choices will affect the movement creation of participants. Unless you are off conceptually in your genesis descriptions, be content with what participants create. Use or don't use the genesis material as God leads. You will grow artistically as you choreograph and participants will expand in their dance choices as they begin to understand the genesis vocabulary.

In genesis sessions, I always have my digital or phone video camera charged up and ready to shoot. If I don't tape the results of genesis, the participants will forget what they design, and I will too. After the first rehearsal, review the recording to see what works and what doesn't work (Review Chapter 3 for tips on successful genesis work).

Literal and non-literal movement

We already know that dance is a universal, non-verbal language. Within this language, two types of movement communicate clearly.

The first type of movement is literal movement. Literal movement copies what a word says. For instance, if someone said, "She is knocking at my door," and this was represented in literal movement, you would actually see a dancer using his or her hand to knock on a real or imagined door. The word door and the action would match exactly.

In Christian dance, I often see the word cross danced with literal movement. It is a wonderful symbol of faith that can be used with strong literal representation. However, be cautious. If an entire dance relies on literal movement, it ceases to be dance. If it is over-used, it produces boring and often predictable movement.

Note other characteristics of literal movement:

1. It is easily identified and understood by the audience.

2. It must be used sparingly, or dance turns into pantomime.

3. It is particularly good for congregational motion prayers and serves as a safety net when participants first enter into dance ministry.

4. With infrequent use, it projects symbolism and imagery in personal and powerful ways.

The second type of movement is non-literal movement. Non-literal movement speaks on its own. A congregation will "get" what you are saying in movement just as they do when they learn another language, as long as you communicate with clear conceptual translation.

How do you do that? If you repeat phrases and verses at the same time that the words of the song repeat, the congregation will connect the words of the song to the movements they see.

Miraculously, they will begin to learn the language of dance. It will talk visually. On the other hand, because it is a language, it must have meaning. That is your job.

As choreographer, you should also feel free to set up a dance with interesting media, lighting, set, prop, written explanation, or costuming components that facilitate the message of the song. Release yourself to do anything that works. Use drama as part of a dance presentation as well. Just make sure that these choices enhance the communication of your identified target. When movement ministry speaks, prayer-in-motion penetrates the soul by blending a variety of access routes.

At its best, you have already learned (through genesis movement and technical phrases) that this non-literal language should develop from an organic base. The designed movement should be created by you from the inside out, and it should be danced from the inside out by participants. In that way it will communicate a biblical concept clearly, and it will personalize the movement with holistic worship. That is the goal of non-literal movement used in dance ministry.

1. It is a new language with endless vocabulary choices.

2. It places biblical concepts into movement clarity.

3. It is a by-product of the technical level of any movement level, and it can be accessed through genesis movement or technical phrases as the choreography base for dance ministry.

4. It speaks authentically when organic movement choices expose faith (in technical or genesis forms) through choreography and personal worship rather than contrived, external choices.

To sum up:
1. Literal movement is used to teach congregational motion prayers and serve as a safety net for process-based beginning motion prayer participants.

2. Non-literal movement vocabulary is used with choreography tools to widen movement vocabulary and to enhance biblical concepts.

In my opinion, you should find yourself moving away from literal movement choices as you choreograph prayer-in-motion. Therefore, non-literal movement should be the main source of your choreography library.

Soul to Sole Step 4

Soul to Sole Step 4: At the first rehearsal, prepare a written handout for the dancers called the movement score: song lyrics, inductive analysis, technical phrases and genesis movement, time signature, choreography target, worship category, biblical research, and a rough outline of where you plan to put your technical phrases and genesis movement.

The first four steps for Soul to Sole Choreography occur before the first rehearsal. Be prepared to teach all technical phrases at the first rehearsal interwoven with genesis creation (that is, if you have decided to use genesis for a particular dance). As you read earlier in my description of technical phrases, sometimes I write out the technical movement with song lyrics; sometimes I don't. It's your choice.

Below is the breakdown for "Who Am I?" by Christy L Nockels and Nathaniel E. Nockels.[55] It reflects the information mentioned for the dance score. I distributed it to dancers at the first rehearsal. This dance was a finalist in a national secular choreography festival.

Dance Score: "Who Am I" by Watermark

Identified biblical concept: Grace. (God's loving grace covers all believers and gives them worth).

Time signature: 4/4

Category: teaching, prayer, and beauty (healing)

B = Believer (one dancer)

HS = Holy Spirit (three dancers)

Verse 1:

Over time you've healed so much in me	B technical #1
And I am living proof	HS genesis

---

[55] WHO AM I, Christy Nockels/Nathan Nockels, ©. 2000 Word Music, LLC, Sweater Weather Music (Admin by Word Music, LLC), Rocketown Music (Admin by Word Music, LLC). All rights reserved. Used by permissions.

That although my darkest hour had come
Your light could still shine through
Though at times it's just enough to cast
A shadow on the wall
Well, I am grateful that you shined your
Light on me at all

CHORUS 1:	B technical #2
Who am I?	HS technical #3
chorus	
*That you would **love** me so gently?*	
Who am I?	
That you would recognize my name?	
Lord who am I?	
That you would speak to me so softly?	
Conversation with the love most high	
Who am I?	
Interlude 16 cts	HS transitional
walking patterns	
Verse 2:	
Well, amazing **grace**	B and one HS dancer technical #1
how sweet the sound	2 HS dancers:
genesis	
that saved a wretch like me	
I once was lost but now am found	
Was blind but now I see	
And the more I sing that sweet old song	
The more I understand	
That I do not comprehend this love	
That's coming from your hand	
CHORUS 1:	
Who am I ?	HS technical #3
chorus	

*That you would **love** me so gently?*	B-responsive

Praise Poses
Who am I?
That you would recognize my name?
Lord who am I?
That you would speak to me so softly?
*Conversation with the **love** most high*
Who am I?

CHORUS 2:

Grace, grace . . . God's **grace**	HS technical #2
Grace that will pardon and cleanse within	B kneeling-

responsive praise poses
Grace, grace . . . God's **grace**
Grace that is greater than all our sin

CHORUS 1:

Who am I?	B & HS (adding in

1 by 1) technical #1
*That you would **love** me so gently?*
Who am I?
That you would recognize my name?
Lord who am I?
That you would speak to me so softly?
*Conversation with the **love** most high*
Who am I?

CHORUS 3:

Amazing grace, how sweet the sound	HS genesis
Amazing love, now flowing down	B responsive praise poses

From hands and feet
That were nailed to the tree
Grace flows down and _covers_ me

CHORUS 3:

Amazing grace, how sweet the sound	HS repeat opening

genesis
Amazing love, now flowing down

From hands and feet
That were nailed to the tree
Grace flows down and _covers_ me

It *covers* me . . . and *covers* me . . .
and *covers* me and . . . *covers* me, yea   Genesis-HS&B
It *covers* me . . . and *covers* me . . .
and *covers* me and . . . *covers* me, yea   ("it"   refers   to
grace]

CHORUS 1:
Who am I?   2   HS   dancers
technical #2
*That you would **love** me so gently?*   B & 1 HS genesis
Who am I?
That you would recognize my name?
Lord who am I?
That you would speak to me so softly?
*Conversation with the **love** most high*
Lord Who am I? Yea
Ooooo.

Inductive Analysis (referring to the lyrics above):

- Chorus 1 is repeated 3x. italics

- Chorus 3 is repeated 2x. bold

- "Grace" is repeated 15x. underlined

- "Love" is repeated 11x. bold ital

- "Covers" is repeated 10x. bold ital. underlined

- "Who am I?" (different font) is repeated 16x with the first chorus repeating the phrase 3x. Therefore, "who am I" has even more significance in this chorus than the other repeated words.

Technical Phrases for Who Am I

Verse 1: (Technical #1) "Over time you've healed so much in me"

Pivot to corner 4 with L ft front [cts 1-2]; step R, L [cts 3, 4] in a circle to end with R foot front lunge to corner 2 [cts 5-8]

"And I am living proof"

Airplane turn to the L with L ft and R foot in attitude [cts 1-4]; step onto R ft as L ft is placed side holding ball of foot in place (corner 2) [cts 5-8]

"That although my darkest hour had come"

Round body over as legs plie low [cts 1-8]

"Your light could still shine through"

Straighten legs as R hand rounds above head [cts 1-4]; step back with L ft [ct 5], then R [ct 6] ending with ft in derriere tendu and arm opening to side [cts 7-8]

"Though at times it's just enough to cast"

Chasse fwd with R ft to corner 2; step walk fwd onto ball of ft-L, R [cts 1-4]; step chasse onto L ft with R in low back attitude; hop 3x in a circle to the L [cts 5-8]

"A shadow on the wall"

Step R to the side to close feet as arms windmill from the L to the R [cts 1-4]; slide lunge L ft to the side and drag closed [cts 5-8]

"Well, I am grateful that you shined your"

Step tendu with L ft to corner 3 as R ft closes to first [cts 1-4]; glissade L ft to close R foot 2x circularly L to face front [cts 5-8].

"Light on me at all"

Cross R ft over L ft [ct 1]; step back onto L ft [ct 2]; coupe to R ft as L ft does a rond de jambe dehors to end in a lunge with the R ft front facing corner 2 [cts 3-8; 1-6]

CHORUS 1 for "Who Am I?": (Technical #2)

"Who am"

Step R, L in a dehors circle with arm circling [cts 7-8]

"I?"

L ft front at ankle as torso lowers [cts 1-4]; change feet so that R ft is at ankle to the front as torso rounds up and L hand opens [cts 5-8] over the head to the side and low

"That you would love me so gently?"

Step R [cts 1-2], L [cts 3-4], R [cts 5-6] in a circle to the L to close in first position facing corner 2 [cts 7-8]

"Who am I?"

Ball change with L ft stepping back as arms roll into body [cts 1-4]; develope side with L foot, ending with L ft on ball of ft side [cts 5-8]; arms open L arm high with R arm side

"That you would recognize my name?"

Rock weight of body to R ft to step chaine turn L [step L, R, cts 1-2]; end with L foot lunge on ball of foot with no arms; look to corner 2 [cts 3-8]

"Lord who am I?"

Step L, R and saute on L as R ft brushes fwd bending to slide under L ft on the ground; L ft does en air switch to back of R foot

"That you would speak to me so softly?"

Brush and circle R hand from low to high [cts 1-2], around the back of the head [cts 3-4] to end with both palms touching each other [cts 5-8]

"Conversation with the love most high"

Slowly stand as arms go to high position above head [cts 1-4]; step with R ft to side lunge as hands open [cts 5-7]; R ft goes to passe [ct 8]

"Who am I?"

Step R [cts 1-2], L [cts 3-4], R [cts 5-6] ft to move in a L circle; hold and twist head around [cts 7-8 and longer as needed]

Finalist presentation of 'Who Am I?' at the Palm Springs National Choreography
Festival in 2004

Genesis Exploration:

1. Using the white skirt that I give you, experiment with six different
   ways to create flowing, sustained movement with the skirt at
   different levels and angles. Use both locomotor and non-
   locomotor movement.

2. In groups of two, design flowing, sustained movements with the
   skirt at different levels and angles using both locomotor and non-
   locomotor movement.

3. Study the definition of grace that is given below and choose four
   descriptive adjectives that come to mind in reference to the
   biblical concept of grace. Using those four descriptive words,
   design two locomotor steps and two non-locomotor steps to create
   a dance phrase from your four word choices to show the group.

Below is some research for "grace" that I used for my own study and
then distributed to the dancers with whom I was working. I asked them to
read it and discuss the concept of "grace" during the rehearsal process in
the opening discussion time of each rehearsal.

Grace is "favor or kindness shown without regard to the worth or merit
of the one who receives it and in spite of what that same person deserves.

Grace is one of the key attributes of God. The Lord God is 'merciful and gracious, long-suffering, and abounding in goodness and truth' (Exodus 34:6). Therefore, grace is almost always associated with mercy, love, compassion, and patience as the source of help and with deliverance from distress.

"In the Old Testament, the supreme example of grace was the redemption of the Hebrew people from Egypt and their establishment in the Promised Land. This did not happen because of any merit on Israel's part, but in spite of their unrighteousness (Deuteronomy 9:5-6). Although the grace of God is always free and undeserved, it must not be taken for granted. Grace is only enjoyed within the covenant—the gift is given by God, and the gift is received by man through repentance and faith (Amos 5:15). Grace is to be humbly sought through the prayer of faith (Malachi 1:9).

"The grace of God was supremely revealed and given in the person and work of Jesus Christ. Jesus was not only the beneficiary of God's grace (Luke 2:40), but He was also its very embodiment (John 1:14), bringing it to mankind for salvation (Titus 2:11). By His death and resurrection, Jesus restored the broken fellowship between God and His people, both Jew and Gentile. The only way of salvation for any person is 'through the grace of the Lord Jesus Christ' (Acts 15:11).

"The grace of God revealed in Jesus Christ is applied to human beings for their salvation by the Holy Spirit, who is called 'the Spirit of grace' (Hebrews 10:29). The Spirit is the One who binds Christ to His people so that they receive forgiveness, adoption to sonship, and newness of life as well as every spiritual gift or grace (Ephesians 4:7).

"The theme of grace is especially prominent in the letters of the apostle Paul. He sets grace radically over against the law and the works of the law (Romans 3:24, 28). Paul makes it abundantly clear that salvation is not something that can be earned or merited; it can be received only as a gift of grace (Romans 4:4). Grace, however, must be accompanied by faith; a person must trust in the mercy and favor of God, even while it is undeserved (Romans 4:16).

"The law of Moses revealed the righteous will of God in the midst of pagan darkness; it was God's gracious gift to Israel (Deuteronomy 4:8).

But His will was made complete when Jesus brought the gospel of grace into the world (John 1:17)."[56]

Although this dance reflected choreographic complexity, the work I did at step 1 simplified the task when I discovered several repeated choruses, verses, and interludes. I also observed that I needed to design two different groups to portray this concept: the believer and a group of three women to represent grace. That analysis led me to create both genesis and technical movement. Was this the only way to do it? No. Did it work? Yes.

Rabbit trail warning 10

Do not wait to put the entire dance together until the fourth rehearsal (or later). Do it at the end of the second rehearsal. This system will protect you and your dancers from stress as you continue the preparation process. In Soul to Sole Choreography, dancers show Christ-based worship the best when they know the movement from start to finish. The learning curve is at the beginning of the process. As rehearsals progress, there will be an increasing attitude of worship along with movement clarity.

Soul to Sole Step 5

Soul to Sole Step 5: Using the choreography tools listed in Chapter 3, continue to design movement for the third and fourth rehearsals to paint a biblical conceptual picture.

The first and second rehearsals are over. During that time, you have taught technical phrases for the dancers to learn and you have given them genesis movement which they have solved with their own movement choices. You have taped this movement material with a video camera or phone. You also know how many dancers will participate in this dance, and you either know or have observed participant movement levels. Last, you have put together the dance in rough form. During the third and fourth rehearsals, review movement tools and ask God to help you focus on the identified choreography target. Begin to craft the final dance.

---

[56] Nelson's Illustrated Bible Dictionary.

Decide when to have dancers enter and exit a dance. Without changing technical phrases or genesis movement, frame them using the backpack of choreography tools (for example, different levels, angles, and pathways). If I have a chorus that repeats four times, sometimes I choreograph two chorus repeats with one technical phrase and two chorus repeats with one genesis phrase. In another dance, I might choreograph the four chorus repeats with two different sets of technical phrases. The possibilities are endless. This doesn't happen automatically. Intentional preparation must occur before you can try ideas at rehearsal. In the past, I rarely set more than a total of six technical phrases or genesis movement for one dance. Usually, I limit myself to the creation of three to five. Once conceptual movement (either genesis or technical) has been created, I continue to re-use the same movement material for most of the dance.

Soul to Sole Step 6

Soul to Sole Step 6: Leave 10-20 percent of the dance choreographically open so that the Spirit can continue to lead the direction of the choreography as you work within the technical level of the participants.

Although new created movement can occur throughout movement design, choreography additions and changes that you set beyond the fourth rehearsal can often confuse and stress your dancers. Preparation is the key. Always continue to pray. Go back to the choreography tools, technical phrases, genesis movement with praise poses, phrases, and explorations.

Rabbit trail warning 11

At a movement roadblock, think about the identified conceptual target and return to it for movement inspiration. Otherwise, you will start creating "movement fluff" (you know, the stuff that you use in every dance when you don't know what to do). As you look to look to the Lord of the dance, the choreography will unfold.

Watch God work in your heart and in the hearts of participants. Enjoy the worship and the dance that God has given you. As you look up to Jesus, rely on Him, and give thanks for His leading. Make sure that you initiate the preview committee to come and see the dance before it is presented (see Chapter 5). And listen to them with humility and respect.

At the end of the rehearsal process, the dance must translate from soul to sole to be prayer-in-motion. This fuses together a presentation level of conceptual communication and technical excellence that demonstrates the reality of faith in Jesus. Based on the six steps of Soul to Sole Choreography, Christian dance ministry can access the heart and can serve as a portal into the soul. Through worship that gives glory to God, the non-verbal language of dance will morph into the literal embodiment of faith.

Ann Stevenson once wrote, "Dance, as we have known it, is a beautiful art form that can pierce the heart, convict and convince, either for good or for evil."[57]

Choreography checklist from Doris Humphrey's The Art of Making Dances:[58]

1. Symmetry is lifeless.

2. Two-dimensional design is lifeless.

3. The eye is faster than the ear.

4. Movement looks slower and weaker on the stage.

5. All dances are too long.

6. A good ending is 40 percent of the dance.

7. Monotony is fatal; look for contrasts.

8. Don't be a slave to, or a mutilator of, the music.

9. Listen to qualified advice; don't be arrogant.

10. Don't intellectualize; motivate movement.

11. Don't leave the ending to the end.

---

[57] Stevenson, 40.

[58] From *The Art of Making Dances* by Doris Humphrey, copyright © 1959 and 1987 by Charles H. Woodford and Barbara Pollock, by permission.

Chapter 5

The Rehearsal Process: Movement Patterns

"Help" describes my best prayer.

It wasn't always that way. During my fifteenth year, I was overwhelmed with life. When I got older, nothing changed. Self-centered rabbit trails blazed everywhere. I didn't know enough about mothering, wife-ing, dancing, cooking or friending (this, before Facebook). What's more, my ears were down if I didn't get my way, and I never got my way. So my life leaked . . . wa-wa-wa. My tear-filled hankie kept waving in the same direction to get God's attention. Prayer with my motion was stuck. Then I had an ah-ha moment: I was turning 'round and 'round in a conversation with myself. It was a solo that should have been a duet.

Jesus never had a chance to ask me to dance because I wasn't interested in His choreography. Unlike the leadership combinations described in Chapter 2, I wasn't in a reciprocal relationship with God. That's when Jesus two-stepped His way into my heart and grabbed it. Patterns turned from crossing rabbit trails to worshiping the Rock. That's why "help" is a wonderful way to start the preparation for Soul to Sole Choreography.

Rehearsal itself becomes a prayer in process that leads to a prayer-in-motion (PIM) presentation.

"The prayer of a righteous person is powerful and effective"
(James 5:16).

REHEARSAL PHILOSOPHY

Prayer to Create the Motion

Get at least one mature Christ-follower who will commit to pray for an upcoming dance in creation and rehearsal. Make sure that you:

1. Ask that person to pray for you daily and make sure that person is not in the dance.

2. Only ask Spirit-led people who understand the importance of prayer.

3. Continue this process during rehearsal and ministry time.

4. Copy this person on all emails/texts having to do with the dance (as well as the pastor or ministry leader).

5. Once rehearsals begin, introduce this person by name to the dancers. Let them know that he or she is available for all prayer requests during the rehearsal of this dance.

> *"I am starting to see there is a difference between 'saying prayers' and honest praying. Both can sound the same on the outside, but the former is too often motivated by a sense of obligation and guilt; whereas the latter is motivated by a conviction that I am completely helpless to 'do life' on my own. Or in the case of praying for others, that I am completely helpless to help others without the grace and power of God."*[59]

Teaching to Reflect the Rock

Do you know that one of your goals during rehearsal is to grow dancers into living stones? First Peter 2:5 says, "You also, like living stones, are being built into a spiritual house, to be a holy priesthood, offering spiritual sacrifices acceptable to God through Jesus Christ."

During the process of rehearsal, go back to Chapter 2 and remember what it means to respond to people instead of react to them. It's all about being Spirit-led and Spirit-filled. Tell yourself the truth about yourself so that you can help your dancers grow in faith and movement as you reflect Jesus. Plan on using a wide range of people and abilities. Living stones may include a group of trained dancers or a rock pile of congregational (untrained) dancers. As you pray in preparation for the first gathering, make sure that you chisel hearts with the following:

---

[59] *A Praying Life*, Paul Miller, 2009, used by permission of NavPress. All rights reserved. www.navpress.com.

1. All dances designed within PIM rehearsal, either with children or adults, should be molded to encourage participants to grow in their understanding of the identified biblical concept.

2. If possible, participants should be allowed to make choices within a warm-up and/or dance to encourage thinking skills and ownership. Use genesis to access the movement base of both trained and untrained dancers. Be clear in your conceptual descriptions to get movement material designed to fit the dance you are working on.

3. The choreographer should take responsibility to make sure each dancer is successful throughout the process of PIM rehearsal unless you are dealing with a dancer that exhibits a bad attitude. A bad attitude needs to be addressed as a separate, individual issue. It is your responsibility to teach in a way that builds movement success. Don't use words to discourage your dancers.

4. Be flexible in your choreography choices. Cut even simple movements that one or more participants can't correctly do and choose new movements that participants can easily execute. Movements that are not done within the technical range of participants distract from a sense of worship and often take the focus off the biblical concept in the dance.

5. People learn movement information in different ways. Some learn motion quickly while others take much longer. Be patient and encourage everybody (including yourself) as you rehearse.

6. Do not encourage faith, movement, or personality comparisons between dancers. Galatians 6:4-5 teaches us, "Each one should test their own actions. Then they can take pride in themselves alone, without comparing themselves to someone else, for each one should carry their own load." This means that each dancer can be used within the technical and personality base he or she possesses to grow spiritually in the rehearsal process. If dancers compare themselves either as better or worse in any area than others, talk to them and work this issue through. Acknowledging

differences in a truthful manner (and even verbalizing them in a rehearsal) is often needed to combat unhealthy comparisons.

Examples:

(a)   One dancer has a Master's in ballet. Another dancer has a technical base just beyond an intermediate level in jazz.

(b)   One dancer comes from a stable Christian home with a responsive heart to Jesus while another dancer comes into dance ministry new to Christ with a rebellious heart and no foundational teaching.

(c)   One dancer is outgoing and one dancer is shy.

We can't begin to compare the two dancers and expect the same maturity and/or abilities from both. On the other hand, it doesn't mean these issues are not addressed during the course of rehearsal. As God leads, you may say nothing related to these issues or you may challenge and exhort a dancer to make some changes. Trust God to help you.

7. The PIM rehearsal covenant (Appendix G) should set high expectations between each living stone dancer and the Lord. Release yourself from feeling bad when other motives for program participation are discovered.

8. Encourage dancers to participate in dance classes and Bible studies to strengthen technical skills and spiritual depth.

Scripture Focus Produces Rock Piles

1. Choose a Scripture to explain the purpose for your dance ministry. In SonLight, the ministry at my church, the key verse is John 12:35b-36: "The man who walks in the dark does not know where he is going. Put your trust in the light while you have it, so that you may become sons of light." Memorize the verse you choose for your group to remind yourself why you are doing what you do. And, as God leads, share that purpose consistently with the

participating living stones in PIM. Group rock piles strengthen dance ministry.

2. Find other ways to incorporate Scripture into the rehearsal process. Don't hesitate to choreograph a verse that highlights the biblical concept being presented. Ask dancers ice-breaker questions about that Scripture. End prayer time with that passage or ask dancers to see how Jesus might teach them about that verse during the week. Discuss their responses at the next rehearsal.

3. Send weekly information to participants that end with Scripture to encourage dancers in their daily walk with the Lord. I change the verses I use on a daily basis, but you can also choose the same one and use it to close all communication.

Scriptural Rock-Piles Produce Healthy Relational Patterns

Try to form healthy rock formations as rehearsals progress:

1. Go for process-based excellence, not performance-based perfectionism. Look to rehearse according to the Rock and His standards, not the world's focus on competition and perfectionism. If you or others need correction in a certain area of your program, pray for help, address the issue with God's heart, and then move forward. The journey of process will mature you and individual dancers as resolution takes place. Everybody can reach the goal of trying their hardest, and everybody can grow in skills. Trust God to work. Relate to dancers as God relates to you, and model growth in a product oriented adult world that needs to see transparency and risk through the process of journeying with the Rock. Increasing skills and exhibiting a spirit of excellence is the goal. Make sure that you understand that a process-based approach is not an excuse to present sloppy, unclear choreography or to not confront relational issues as they come up in your leadership.

2. Stop gossip. Often, neither believers nor non-believers go to the person with whom they are having difficulty. Most of the time, they talk to everyone but that person. That is not scriptural.

Matthew 18:15 instructs us, "If your brother or sister sins, go and point out their fault, just between the two of you. If they listen to you, you have won them over."

3. When people come to me with relational trouble, I share this rule: If I am not part of the problem or part of the solution, I challenge people to share the information that they discuss with me with the person who is involved. This should be the first step to resolve any relational issue. I do prayerfully respond to someone who wants godly input, but I keep the information confidential unless I am given permission to share it. Then I agree with that person to love and to pray for the situation and the person(s) involved. This is an example of bearing burdens with fellow Christians, which leads believers to express agape love (Galatians 6:2).

4. Understand the importance of submission addressed at the end of Chapters 2 and 6. Always speak the truth in love, especially if there are differences of opinion. We need truth in our discussions. Be responsive, not reactive. If there is a leader over you, and a decision is made that you disagree with, follow his or her leadership with respect and with a sweet spirit. Evaluate the attitude in your heart, and watch for sin from yourself. Follow the same guidelines when you are the leader and you have a dancer who does not agree with a leadership decision you make. Christ wants to see if you honor Him whether you agree with someone or whether someone agrees with you. Trust the God who judges justly (1 Peter 2:23).

5. Do feel free to openly discuss a ministry concern with a dancer who comes to you with a question; that may evolve into educating dancers with a group discussion. Focus on the issue, not people. Always use a scriptural foundation for answers.

Leadership Lookout

Others should be given leadership opportunities if their strength is knowing God, listening to the Holy Spirit, and loving God and others. Their actions should reflect a growing awareness of themselves with an ability to self-correct sinful behaviors. These are participants who usually have a good attitude, express a call into dance ministry, model servanthood and obedience, and submit to leadership. Make sure that all dancers involved in ministry leadership understand the leadership philosophy, sign the leadership covenant, and communicate openly with the ministry leader above them. Watch God build "living stones" to His glory through you and dance ministry.

Weight-Watching Rocks

Our culture values outward physical form rather than inner character content in dancers. A skinny dancer doesn't necessarily mean a better dancer (although it's just fine if that is a particular person's body type). Don't allow the group or individual participants to focus on weight issues. I encourage people to eat healthy and exercise regularly to take care of body stewardship. All body types and all body weights should be welcomed into dance ministry if they fulfill the participant requirements.

SOUL TO SOLE PREVIEW STANDARDS

Pastors and church staff must have standards for what they do and so must those in dance ministry if the art form is to be taken seriously. To develop dance criteria that aligns with God's heart, establish a group of strong Christ-followers who will come into the latter part of the rehearsal process to preview a dance and tell you what they see communicated in words and movement. Can they identify the biblical concept in the dance without being prompted?

- Use believers who speak the truth with a Spirit-led heart, not friends who tell you what you want to hear.
- Use believers who know the Word in depth and who are committed to living in obedience to Christ.
- Use believers who are not afraid to address gender issues (for example, erotic costumes or movements).

How do we set up this kind of group?

- Get input from the ministry leader with whom you are working. I recommend elders to be part of this group, people who are in full-time Christian service, and/or respected members of the church.
- Send out a letter to this group explaining the goal of previewing a dance and invite them to be a part of the preview process.
- Plan for two to four people to view PIM one to two weeks before it is presented for ministry. Be prepared to cancel the dance if it does not pass preview standards.
- Make sure that those who are on this committee understand they evaluate the dance based on an identifiable biblical concept in the music or text, costume, and movement choice (See preview letter below).
- These volunteers do not have to be arts-oriented people. However, they must be comfortable using the arts, specifically dance, as a worship and communication tool.
- If you need to, address the issue of erotic choices openly in evaluation. Movement, garment, and music selections must be modest. If you are embarrassed (or afraid) to discuss any area of the dance that needs to be evaluated, you are probably not ready to direct a motion prayer group.
- If there is a purposeful reason for two people of the opposite gender to have physical contact in a duet, rehearse with a chaperone.
- In choreography, the primary level of evaluation must be that the movement does not contradict the biblical concept portrayed in the text. This still allows for countless creative choices within appropriate boundaries.

Evaluation in the arts is tricky because success or failure is subjective. It is through the process of identifying a worship category and a biblical concept prior to choreographing PIM that we have a clear goal. When we start the choreography process with a clear goal, we increase the chances for successful movement design.

Invitation Letter for Dance Preview

Dear --------,

Greetings in the name of the Lord! I am honored to write you this letter, and I do so on behalf of SonLight prayer-in-motion at Trinity Church. SonLight is a ministry of the arts that uses movement as a non-verbal tool to share the Gospel of Jesus Christ through the worship of those involved in a particular dance. Part of God's direction for this ministry has been to ask men and women of faith to come into the rehearsal process to view the motion prayer before it is presented to the congregation.

Each dance that you see is purposefully chosen and prayerfully considered prior to rehearsal.

I hope that you have been blessed by this ministry. However, I believe that to maintain God's standards and not my own, SonLight is called to invite mature Christ-followers into the rehearsal process to make sure that dance speaks biblically into the hearts of those watching.

I would love to have you on the list of those Christ-followers willing to serve in this capacity. This would involve the following:

1. *To read chapter one from Dance is Prayer-in-Motion. That chapter defines the philosophy and goals of prayer-in-motion for the dance ministry at this church. Note that each dance should communicate a biblical concept.*

2. *To come to one of the last rehearsals of a dance and view the dance to determine if it succeeds as a ministry tool leading believers and non-believers to be drawn to the Lord Jesus.*

3. *To give honest feedback to the choreographer as well as the group involved in the movement. Ephesians 4:15 asks believers to "speak the truth in love."*

4. *To fill out a dance preview form.*

5. *No movement skills or background is necessary. FAITH is the critical factor.*

6. *If you choose to place yourself on this list, the person setting up your involvement might call you one or two times a year. If you cannot come to a rehearsal, all you have to do is say no.*

7. *Call _____ to let me know of your involvement.*

8. *If you have any questions or concerns, feel free to give me a personal call.*

9. *As God leads you, pray for the motion prayer you have viewed.*

Thank you for considering this very special involvement in dance ministry.
much love,

Mary Bawden
For you: "And whatever you do, whether in word or deed, do it all in the name of the Lord Jesus, giving thanks to God the Father through him" (Colossians 3:17).

Overall Evaluation

Listed below are the patterns for the preview committee to consider (with the * as the most important):

1. What kind of response did I have to the dance?

2. Did the dance enhance worship through praise, beauty, teaching, celebration, or prayer?

3. Did the choreography communicate biblical truth through an identified biblical concept in the song or text? Did you see that concept in the overall scope of the movement?*

4. Was the technical level crafted so that the movement was clearly and cleanly presented?

5. Was there erotic movement, song, or costume choice?

6. Was there anything else—weak or strong—included in this dance that made it stand out?

7. Did the dancers express worship with their bodies: heart, mind, and soul?

The evaluations that come from the preview committee are a crucial aspect of Soul to Sole Choreography. Truthful speech (Ephesians 4:15) will prevent some dances from being presented. Sometimes comments will allow for necessary corrections in costuming, music, and movement choices with one additional evaluation preview. On the other hand, when previews support a created ministry dance, a choreographer and dancers can use that encouragement to enter into ministry with congregational and pastoral assurance. Take the preview seriously, have a good attitude, and use it for growth as you increase your skills. *The dance preview form is found in Appendix H.*

PRE-REHEARSAL PROCESS

Pre-rehearsal requirements to participate in PIM:

- Christian-life yielded to the Lordship of Jesus or seekers as pastoral staff permits.

- Ongoing technical preparation at the individual level of participation.

- Fulfill the requirements of rehearsal covenant.

- Requirements of a particular church, e.g. trained dancers must have dance training beyond a beginning level, etc.

Pre-Rehearsal Critical Trio: Welcome Letter, Mailer, and Rehearsal Covenant

A. Welcome letter

(Should be sent to new dancers before the first rehearsal. Outline the philosophy and structure of the program so that each dancer understands ministry expectations and goals):

Dear dancer, Welcome to prayer-in-motion (PIM)! This letter is written to you specifically because this is the first time that you will be participating at ____Church using your gifts in prayer-in-motion. We are excited to get to know you and to have you develop friendships with all the members involved in dance ministry.

You should know the following:

1. *PIM is a process program that ends in a product, which is presented. There is not a competitive focus in PIM but rather an attitude of grace and process-based excellence. God allows this program to flourish so that we end up with beautiful presentations that minister to the congregation. Relax. There are men and women who have a variety of technical levels in this program. You will fit in at your own movement level. Trust us on this!*

2. *Enclosed is a copy of the PIM covenant. Read it carefully. Every time a motion prayer is planned, all who participate in it sign the covenant for that particular prayer-in-motion. When the dance has been presented, the covenant you sign is completed. We ask that you take the covenant seriously. After you read it, feel free to call with any questions. All conversations will be confidential.*

3. *Dress modestly. What does that mean? In SonLight (replace this with your group name), it means loosely fitted clothing. There should be no tank tops, bare mid-riff, tight pants, etc. Often, untrained members wear loose t-shirts and shorts, or sweat-pants. Because SonLight II members have a trained technical base, we often work in rehearsal using a modest leotard, tights (nothing high-cut in the leg area, low cut in the bust area, or styled with string exposure for the derriere, etc.) and leg warmers as well as sweat-pants (especially when it's cold). If there is male participation in a trained dance rehearsal, ladies wear a loose t-shirt over their leotard. Feel free to wear ballet shoes if you wish. However, many leaders work in bare feet and choreograph with that in mind. Do what is comfortable for you.*

4. *There are usually five to seven weeks (six to 10 rehearsals) to learn the dances. However, do keep open to optional rehearsals as they are needed. More importantly, understand that with the rehearsal covenant you will actually have 35 rehearsals of a particular dance. If there are five weeks of rehearsal scheduled, five weeks of preparation times seven days per week equals 35 rehearsals. In the covenant, you are encouraged to practice the*

dance one time per day. PIM does this so that the rehearsed dance is not "steps that we perform" but worship given to the Lord Jesus. It is the high level of worship in PIM that allows the program to minister to others as well as ourselves.

a. *The first rehearsal focuses on what I call "technicals." These are the movement phrases used over and over in the dance. They need to be practiced after the first rehearsal and learned completely so that the second rehearsal is successful. Genesis material is also created and taped at this rehearsal.*

b. *We call our second meeting "the rough cut" rehearsal. The goal of this meeting is to complete the entire dance from start to finish with the phrases learned at the first rehearsal with a spatial awareness of how the dance will progress. It is normal to feel a bit overwhelmed at this point as everything is new and it feels messy (just ask anybody who has been in a dance).*

c. *At the third/fourth rehearsal, we make "jello." It is aptly called the "jello rehearsal." The dance really begins to take shape (at least sections). We spend time on detail at last! SonLight members really begin to get a sense of what we're doing.*

d. *The fifth to the dress rehearsals work on detail and any changes that need to be made.*

e. *The last rehearsal is done in full dress attire with lights, sound, and media as needed.*

Because each dance is a creation of its own, you need to understand that the group needs to be flexible. SonLight does not operate like a movement class. Although the choreographer comes into the process very prepared, rehearsal develops individually according to the group that is participating and with the leading of the Holy Spirit. Often, the end product is based on the movement vocabulary of those in the dance. Please be patient with us and with other dance members as God shows us what and who works best for a particular section in the dance. Most of all, be expectant to see God work and TRUST Him in the process.

We start and finish right on time. The structure of the rehearsal time begins with prayer and moves into an ice-breaker question (in which we all have a short time to share). This allows all of the dance ministry members in a particular dance to get to know each other. Then we move into warm-up exercises, which are designed to prevent injury and even more important, to lead all of us into worship before we work on the dance. Often, we quickly choreograph Scripture that is thematic to the biblical concept. When warm-ups are completed, we move right into the dance itself and work on it until approximately 10 minutes prior to the end of rehearsal. We often close our rehearsal with prayer.

PIM is a worship ministry that bases its choreography on biblical concepts. We do this by an inductive analysis of the movement text. We find the message that we want to convey, and then we try to design that into the visual picture of what we are doing. The first rehearsal you will receive notes for the dance as well as an understanding of the biblical concept we're working on. Otherwise, we can end up doing movement "stuff" that conveys no meaning, or we can be "pretty" or "strong" for no reason.

To get to know you better, please answer these questions at the bottom of this letter and return them prior to or at the first rehearsal:

What is your background in faith?

When did you come to know the Lord personally? It is fine to be brief. You may also include any other information that you would like to share with us.

Expect weekly communication during the duration of the dance. We try to communicate with you clearly so that there is no confusion as to what is happening during the rehearsal process of a dance. We also hope to encourage the group and to answer questions that come up! Please leave us with your full mailing address, phone number, and email address before or after the first rehearsal. Check your email/text address weekly during the duration of rehearsals.

Finally, you need to understand the importance of the rehearsal covenant that is signed by all participants at the scheduling session during the first rehearsal. In that first meeting, the group decides on the rehearsals for an upcoming dance based on their personal schedules (including the schedule of the choreographer). All participants have input into this process since every participant brings his or her personal calendar to this rehearsal. However, once everyone agrees upon these rehearsal dates, you are making a verbal and signed agreement to be present for each scheduled dance rehearsal (unless sickness or a family death occur). When an absence occurs, the entire group needs to decide when to plan an additional rehearsal because the choreographer needs each scheduled rehearsal to complete a ministry project in the allotted time. In rare cases, we have had to drop dancers from a dance because they did not honor the rehearsal requirements to be in a ministry presentation. We have only seven to 10 mandatory rehearsals to create and rehearse a motion prayer. Your absence at any rehearsals leaves not only the movement designed for you undone, but also creates stress for the choreographer and the other dancers. And, missing a rehearsal allows other dancers permission to do the same thing during future rehearsals. By the grace of God, this program has been able to develop, create, and rehearse what we do quickly with little stress and worshipful release that ministers at high levels to those who watch. No-shows at rehearsals are never an option. We have clarified this philosophy so as to communicate the importance of the signed rehearsal covenant. SonLight has not had difficulties in ministry because we try to communicate clearly as people enter into the program. If you do not understand this explanation or if you have questions, please feel free to call or email the choreographer about the dance in which you are involved.

The covenant also contains a release form that has been recommended by other Christian arts people. Sometimes we share dances with other sources. As a result, we have compiled DVD collections that represent examples of movement communicating biblical messages. The dance you just signed up for may or may not be used in this capacity. If it is, we want to have a release in place that allows us to do this without confusion. If you have questions regarding this aspect of PIM, please feel free to ask for clarification.

We are excited to see you at the first rehearsal. We are praying for both you and the dance that God will show us!

much love,

Mary Bawden

"The man who walks in the dark does not know where he is going. Put your trust in the light while you have it, so that you may become sons of light" (John 12:35b-36).

Your name:

What is your background in faith?

When did you come to know the Lord personally?

B. Mailer

Send out an email letter with all the pertinent information about a new dance. In that email, invite dancers to participate in the ministry opportunity. Tell them the presentation date along with the time of the first rehearsal.

In your initial mailer, ask participants to call, email, or text you to let you know of their desire to be in the dance as soon as possible. This allows the choreographer to prepare movement material with a certain number of people in mind. Be content with who responds. If a dancer enters the rehearsal process with an attitude that he or she has done the choreographer a favor, it sets a tone of freedom to be late to rehearsal, to miss rehearsal, and any other number of other carnal attitudes.

At the end of the first rehearsal, set up rehearsals based on dancer schedules. Then have all dancers sign the rehearsal covenant (Appendix G), which clarifies the priorities in the rehearsal process.

Particularly critical is rehearsal attendance. I emphasized rehearsal attendance in the welcome letter, and I will repeat that emphasis here. A dancer can miss a rehearsal if he or she is seriously ill or because of a death. However, dancers need to know that a new rehearsal must be scheduled if someone misses. Rehearsals cannot be changed unless all of the dancers agree to a change. Sometimes I've had to drop a dancer from a presentation because of the lack of commitment to come to rehearsal once he or she has signed the covenant and agreed to specific times and dates. A choreographer cannot successfully complete a prayer-in-motion target when there is partial rehearsal attendance.

However, there is one exception to this rule. The date and time of the first rehearsal has the potential to prevent an interested dancer from being present based on prior commitments. The first rehearsal is not scheduled with group agreement so it is valid if a dancer can't attend the first meeting. Therefore, for the dancer who is interested and unavailable for that rehearsal, there is an option. I allow a dancer to send a personal schedule to me so that I have it during the scheduling session (where the rehearsal covenant is signed) during the first rehearsal. Sometimes I can work that dancer into the rehearsal schedule as we calendar and sometimes I can't. If there are unsolvable conflicts between a dancer who cannot attend and the group who is physically present, the priority goes to the dancers that are physically present. And, of course, I meet with individual dancers who miss the first session prior to the next rehearsal so they are caught up and have mastered the material shared at the first rehearsal. This structure works because each dancer is learning technical phrases individually at the first rehearsal. A dancer can also be added into genesis material by having them do the same movement that one other dancer has created from the initial calendaring session. If the genesis material allows for this, they can also solve genesis by themselves.

The rehearsal covenant is one of many reasons that PIM dance ministry is not chaotic and produces dance ministry that communicates the gospel. Many dance programs crash because they don't insist on a signed rehearsal covenant with mandatory attendance.

Sample of a mailer

Greetings in the name of the Lord! I am excited to let you know of a new dance that will be presented on Saturday, October 10, at the annual Christian concert held at Trinity Church at 4:00 p.m. The presentation will also be shared in church services on the next day, October 11, during all three services.

This particular dance will be spectacular in that it will combine the beauty of dance and media to reveal the glory of God. This will be done with screen projection above the dance. Our media team will project slides onto the screen at different times in the dance. The content of the slides will be drawn from our media library and will be specifically chosen to reflect the concept that Pastor Gary preaches on for that Sunday, which is the glory of God. SonLight will dance to a beautiful song by Sandi Patti called "You Alone," which captures God's glory conceptually. The song is upbeat as well as descriptive and reverent. SonLight is really blessed to share it with the congregation and at the Christian dance concert.

Here's the scoop: The first rehearsal is on Saturday, September 5, from 3:00-5:00 p.m. in L213. At the end of the first rehearsal, we will schedule the rest of the rehearsals for this dance.

PRESENTATIONS:

1. *Saturday, October 10, 4:00 p.m. Run-through with media in the morning.*

2. *Sunday, October 11, 8:00, 9:30, and 10:30 a.m. Be at church at 6:30 a.m.; run-through in the sanctuary at 7:15 a.m.*

Call, text, or email on or before September 1 to let me know of your involvement.
much love, Mary.

For you: "The heavens declare the glory of God; the skies proclaim the work of his hands. Day after day they pour forth speech; night after night they display knowledge. There is no speech or language where their voice is not heard. Their voice goes out into all the earth, their words to the ends of the world" (Psalm 19:1-4).

C. Rehearsal covenant

The Rehearsal Covenant: Dance Member Covenant (also found in Appendix G)

I wish to participate at _____ Church honoring the Lord Jesus through prayer-in-motion.
I agree to the following:

1. *Mandatory rehearsal as designated by dance ministry participants.*

2. *The desire to share the Gospel through the visual arts.*

3. *A heart that would encourage rather than discourage as well as the commitment to speak the truth-in-love when it is necessary.*

4. *Confidentiality of personal prayer requests shared.*

5. *A commitment to pray for those participating in this dance as well as for those who watch.*

6. *An encouragement to study the Bible daily so as to be sensitive to God's personal life direction as well as His leading in the design of the motion prayer being rehearsed.*

7. *A pledge of moral purity as taught in Scripture.*

8. *A commitment to check out a CD or listen to the song on an IPOD or Internet connection with an encouragement to practice the worship dance being rehearsed at least one time per day until it is shared.*

9. *Release: I authorize unlimited use of my photograph along with any ministry dances in which I have participated. I waive any claim for compensation. I also waive any right to inspect the finished work or approve the use to which it may be applied. I certify that I fully understand the meaning of this release and because I intend for it to be legally binding, I am signing this sheet.*

Date: _____

Name of Dance: _____

Names of Participants: _____

1.

2.

3.

4.

Critical Trio Summary

A. Send out the Welcome Letter to first-time participants, outlining the philosophy and structure of the program so that each person understands ministry expectations and goals.

B. Send out the initial mailer followed by weekly emails/texts.

C. Present the Rehearsal Covenant at the first rehearsal and ask participants to sign it after dance rehearsals have been scheduled.

REHEARSAL STRUCTURE

Two-Hour Rehearsal

Prayer and ice-breaker (15 minutes)

Chapter 1 emphasized the meaning of worship that gives glory to God. In PIM and in daily actions, it is easy to forget that worshiping Jesus is the purpose for rehearsals, for presentation, and for life responses. You can't control the heart attitudes of the dancers, but you can choose a rehearsal structure that fertilizes the soil for internal choices honoring Jesus. A good leader provides the right rehearsal structure to encourage personal growth and communion with God. A good leader challenges a carnal atmosphere. Start with prayer and then ask the dancers an icebreaker question. No one should be forced to share. Begin this time with whimsical, fun questions (favorite dessert, etc.). Later, use the biblical concept being choreographed as an inductive question—What challenges you about this concept? What is God teaching you this week about this biblical concept? Use phrases in the song to stimulate discussion. Finally, pray specifically for God's direction as the dance progresses. After this prayer and initial sharing, prepare to rehearse the dance with movement warm-ups.

Warm-ups (15 minutes)

Warm-ups are an intentional quiet time to engage with God and worship Him. This section of PIM rehearsal should be used to give glory to God by warming up the body for PIM as dancers wrap their hearts around Jesus. In a world of noise, ask your dancers to spend time in worship before you actually rehearse the dance. There should be no talking. This is a time for the Holy Spirit to move.

During a warm-up, dancers can personally pray, they can listen for the voice of the Holy Spirit, they can meditate on a Scripture verse that you have on the board, they can cry out for help, or they can actively choose to reflect a quiet heart in the warm-up in any way that God directs.

This rehearsal section is similar to the worship time in a church service. Talking with others or eating takes away from honoring Jesus. I have never directed a rehearsal without needing this time to re-focus my thoughts or the thoughts of the dancers on Jesus. Author Gordon MacDonald once wrote, "If my private world is in order, it will be because I am convinced that the inner world of the spiritual must govern the outer world of activity."[60]

Choose music selections for warm-ups with the same criteria used when music is chosen for choreography selection (See Chapter 4 for details). Inductively analyze the music text to identify a biblical concept and listen carefully for clarity of sung words. Feel free to create warm-up movement that could include a phrase from technical phrase material of the song you choreograph. It's also important to use warm-up technique that all participants can achieve.

1. Teach warm-ups at the first rehearsal. Verbalize them again at the second rehearsal. After that, encourage dancers to do the warm-up at their own meter so that they enter into worship with the Lord Jesus. If they have forgotten either one, invite dancers to copy you.

2. If the warm-up is too technical for the group involved, a high frustration level develops that leads the participants away from worship. They tend to feel defective instead of prepared as they enter the dance rehearsal process.

3. Set a personal tone that is non-competitive and encourage, encourage, encourage.

---

[60] MacDonald, 12.

4. Always make sure that warm-up design includes stretches in the following areas: torso, Achilles tendon, and hamstring muscles. Emphasize core control during all warm-ups.

5. As warm-ups are designed, create them with an awareness of the movement bases of the group rehearsing a movement prayer.

6. Although the warm-up should be simple, create it thoughtfully.

Create two choreographed warm-ups for each new dance project. Use the same warm-ups for the duration of the dance. Feel free to use technical movement as a base for one warm-up and structured improvisation for another one.

Example 1: stand in parallel position; roll down to the floor with the head leading the movement; roll up from the floor with the head last; walk eight counts anywhere; choose a praise pose to freeze in and release the pose; repeat this structure in individual metered time until music is finished.

Example 2: all participant choices can be on any level, in any direction; this warm-up used a piece of music that lasted 10 minutes so it was the only one we used.

Section 1: take a shape based on how your day went; stretch one part of the shape in the opposite direction.

Section 2: follow leader in a structured warm-up phrase that he or she has designed.

Section 3: choose non-locomotor movements (anchored movements: twist/turn, curl/stretch, bend/straighten, swing/rock) as you wish.

Section 4: design "stillness" in a praise pose of choice (with an encouragement to use this time for confession and prayer).

Section 5: choose to do any series of locomotor movement except walking OR design a frozen shape of choice (for those who choose a frozen shape, other participants can choose to touch them in an appropriate place to remind them of Christ's touch in their lives). Participants can go in and out of stillness or locomotor movement.

Section 6: choose a way to gently stretch your body in a way you choose OR follow the stretch of another person.

Section 7: locomotor walk section—change direction in from 1-8 counts OR stop and do slow arm movements for as long as you want which anyone can choose to follow for as long as they want. At any time, participants can go back into the walking structure.

Example 3: Have the rehearsing dancers share favorite warm-up movements. List them as they are suggested on the board. Add one last suggestion called "fill in the blank." Each dancer can choose any warm-up movement he or she wants to do in this section. Put on beautiful music and have the group go through the order of ideas on the board. Stay in each section as long as each dancer wants. Everyone can worship and warm-up in his or her own meter.

Rehearse the dance with corrections (1.5 hours)

For maximum understanding, use a board to write corrections. Dancers can see and hear what needs to change in the creative process. Be aware of how people learn differently.

Allow movement corrections to be processed in the rehearsal space with an open time of question and answer as the group needs.

Once dancers go to the sanctuary to rehearse, allow them to process the corrections with as much quietness as possible. Encourage dancers to worship in rehearsal, especially when the dance is set. Focus on worship not performance. This attitude will carry into the ministry presentation.

Schedule of Rehearsals

Schedule seven to 10 mandatory rehearsals for each PIM.

Rehearsal #1: Teach technical phrases and create genesis movement. Distribute detailed movement notes and music CDs for practice at the first rehearsal; have participants sign the covenant.

Rehearsal #2: Complete the dance during the second rehearsal. When you insert genesis material into the dance, cue your video to the genesis phrases you plan to use so that participants can remember what they created during the first rehearsal. Use the sanctuary space to run-through the dance and record the rehearsal so that space and movement corrections can be clearly identified for the third rehearsal. At the chaotic second rehearsal, when you put the entire dance together, everyone is trying to remember what to do in what section of the dance (use your dance score to help). Focus on process and assure participants to do the best they can at this stage. In the music sections that you have not yet designed, have participants improvise movement with praise poses, etc. Resist the urge to answer detailed movement questions. Putting the dance together quickly will ultimately result in a peaceful atmosphere by the end of the choreography process as dancers worship Jesus.

Rehearsals #3-4: Make "jello" (clarify and work on details of different sections) during these two rehearsals. Run the entire dance with corrections.

Rehearsals #5-9: Polish and focus on worship as the dance is finished. Preview committee comes into the rehearsal for dance evaluation.

Final Rehearsal: Lights, sound, media, props, and choreography elements are completed and rehearsed as they will be done for the final presentation.

Optional Rehearsals

Schedule optional rehearsals as needed. These rehearsals are necessary because I find group members always want them. I used to work individually with people (and sometimes still do). However, I have found that everyone benefits if an optional rehearsal has several people there. If someone does need individual rehearsal, ask him or her to come one hour early to rehearsal.

Weekly Email/Text

Send a weekly letter to all participants with administrative details, encouragement, and biblical teaching. Do not allow the actual rehearsal time to be spent on administrative details. This will lead the group away from a sense of worship and onto rabbit trails that will take away from the creation process.

Sample of a weekly administrative letter:

Greetings in the name of our Lord! I was really delighted at what we accomplished during the rehearsal on Saturday. Thank you for moving into the music and the combinations so quickly. I experienced grace as I watched you in the movement and as you allowed me to teach so swiftly. I look forward to this Saturday as we put the entire dance together. Make sure that you continue to covenant and have the choreography clearly in your mind. Plan not to be overwhelmed as we complete the dance and move through all the dance phrases.

I met with the media team on Monday morning at 9:00 a.m. We had a wonderful meeting. I got a practical idea as to the spacing of the slide projectors. Do pray for flexibility for both our group and for the media team as this motion prayer unfolds. Continue to meditate on the concept of glory.

Here is some additional information that I did not have time to cover on Saturday, which should help us prepare for the dance.

Doxa (glory)—in secular Greek, this means opinion or reputation.

There are several ways the Bible describes the glory of God. In the New Testament, the shepherds view it at the birth of Christ, and then by His disciples during His incarnate life. The resurrection and ascension are also seen as manifestations of His glory. Its chief use is to describe the revelation of the character and the presence of God in the person and work of Jesus Christ. He is the outshining of divine glory (Hebrews 1:3).

This week search for favorite Bible verses relating to the glory of God. At our upcoming rehearsal, come prepared to share what you discovered, relating how that truth affects your life right now.

May God continue to teach all of us about his glory. I pray that our lives would reflect that glory with new depth as we rehearse and pray about "You Alone."

much love, Mary.

For you: "The Son is the radiance of God's glory and the exact representation of his being, sustaining withal things by his powerful word. After he had provided for the sins of mankind, he sat down in heaven at the right side of God, the Supreme Power" (Hebrews 1:3).

Additional Rehearsal Tips

1. Use a digital video camera/phone to record each rehearsal so that you can have concise corrections ready for the next rehearsal. A video sees details that you can't always focus on during a rehearsal.

2. Plan on several hours of reflection after each rehearsal with the concept you are developing as the primary focus. Resist the temptation to design "cool movement stuff" that is not concept enhancing.

3. Never come into rehearsal unprepared. Even as you try ideas, come with them in mind.

4. Have audio CDs of the dance to be handed out at the first rehearsal with movement notes. These are great for the dancers but even better for you. You'll remember what you create and plan.

5. Reserve rehearsal space prior to the start of all rehearsals.

6. Be godly in your response to janitorial staff whether you get what you want or not. Make sure they know your rehearsal schedule. Never leave trash for them to pick up. Ask the janitorial staff if you need to improve in any area. Thank them continually.

7. Make sure to send a rehearsal schedule to any tech people who do sound and lights during the presentation. Be kind and encourage them with suggestions as God leads.

8. Don't hesitate to include a brief explanation of a dance in the church bulletin. If your movement communication is clear, many people will understand it. However, some people will not understand the non-verbal language of dance. Audio tape explanations work well too.

9. Try to have mirrors installed in the room your group gathers in during warm-ups and prayer. This allows dancers to see corrections immediately. If your rehearsal space is the sanctuary, it probably won't have mirrors. That's an additional reason to record all rehearsals so that you can show rehearsal challenges to dancers early in the practices.

10. Note who is downstage at different times during the dance; since all participants can see this individual, have that person lead the movement phrases for the rest of the group.

11. Make sure dancers understand how important it is to show the worship of Jesus facially. Remind your dancers of the importance of practicing the dance at least one time per day. It will turn any level of movement into worship. Try not to make changes at the last moment. Choreography accompanied by unresponsive, stiff, or worried faces does not demonstrate worship from the heart. Directing a dance group of any technical level and creating worshipers who dance for Jesus are two separate issues. Be clear in your expectations to grow worshipers.

12. Make sure that you encourage people of all ages to participate in dance ministry. Don't forget to invite participants in their 50s, 60s, 70s, and beyond. Seeing a wide variety of ages and genders allows all Christ-followers to see worship that encourages them to continue the race and finish well.

13. Look in Appendix I for the timeline of deadlines for church choreographers that occur within the rehearsal process. Use or don't use them as they apply to the dance ministry at your church.

REHEARSAL CONSIDERATIONS

Ron Richards portrays his struggle with sin in 'You Have Me'

Men in Choreography

We need men to portray some aspects of conceptual biblical choreography. When we choreograph dances using women for all concepts, we present a partial picture of how God moves in the lives of His people. Half of the audience can't identify with a concept if we ALWAYS use women to portray it. How would you relate to the characters in a movie if they were always men or always women?

Carefully consider which songs indicate the use of men. Listen to the song choice and invite men into the dance depending on the biblical concept as well as the arrangement of the song. Women cannot conceptualize strength and power like a man. A man's height, frame, and muscles naturally project strength and power. Likewise, women can portray softness and lyricism better than men through natural beauty, frame, and innate sensitivity. Both genders are needed to present a full picture of biblical messages.

Look for men who are Christ-followers of deep faith. They risk more and are not intimidated by involvement in dance ministry if you are sensitive to their masculinity. The choreographer must create movements for them that are not feminine. Do not dress men in garments that are soft and lyrical. A confident man instinctively knows when movement is not masculine. Access their movement base by using genesis so that their movements are organic.

Lighting, Props, Set, Video, and Space

Set design for 'Center' with Jerry Flasschoen and Mary Bawden

Feel free to use props, lighting, sets, video and space (processionals, recessionals, and aisles) that will enhance the choreographic goal of a dance. Flags, ribbons, tambourines, garlands, banners, videos, props, set design, and flowing material make wonderful additions. Be open to new ideas. Just make sure that whatever you use doesn't draw others away from worshiping Jesus. I have often seen additions that don't enhance the goal of the choreography.

Using a video background during 'Architecture' presentation

Mary Bawden Checklist

In every dance, remember:

- ✓ There are choreographic exceptions to every rule.

- ✓ Trust the Holy Spirit to guide you. Really.

- ✓ Invest in the process and be content with disappointment in choreography results. You'll get better. Participants will get better. The product will improve and the process will get better.

✓ Keep trying. Understand that you at your weakest point have a message of hope that is stronger than any secular world message.

✓ Study the Word of God continually and in depth.

✓ Make sure that you have personal accountability in your own personal walk with Christ. Friends who don't challenge you in sinful areas are not good choices.

✓ Confront yourself at the personal level when your actions are inconsistent with Scripture and allow God to change you and grow you into the person He wants you to be. Don't focus on changing everyone else. Allow God to do that.

✓ Don't be surprised if you feel attacked by the enemy. Ignore feelings of discouragement and look to Christ in hope.

✓ I do sometimes use the word dance as I work in prayer-in-motion. This is because it is a word most people have in their vocabulary. Of course, the Bible uses the word dance as well. However, our culture uses the word dance in an entirely different context. That is why I feel it is important to distinguish between the two labels.

✓ Fear often invades the process of choreography. Confess your fear with a trusted friend and continue the ministry journey.

✓ Use every opportunity in your personal walk with God to laugh in a wholesome way (Proverbs 17:22a).

✓ Don't discount movement ideas that God gives you as you create a dance. Try them and trust the Spirit's prompting. Many of the most effective ideas I have used in dances are ideas that I initially rejected.

✓ As you choreograph, continue to focus on the biblical concept that has been revealed through the organic analysis of the text. DO NOT ALLOW YOURSELF TO FOCUS ON PLEASING THE SECULAR NEEDS OF PARTICIPANTS WHO MIGHT PRESSURE YOU TO USE CERTAIN COSTUMES, CERTAIN MUSIC, CERTAIN SOLO MOVEMENTS, ETC. The only foundation base for any choice in a motion prayer must be the enhancement of the biblical concept. Otherwise, the choreography process will produce "movement stuff." As believers, we are to please God, not people. This does not mean that you don't get healthy input from participants as you ask or as they suggest. It simply means that the base of what you use or don't use must come from God's leading and not participant pressure.

✓ Make sure that dance participants understand the importance of transforming dance steps into worship. Secular arts people "perform" onstage. Although PIM can sometimes look like an arts performance, we are not involved in ministry executing skills to glorify ourselves. We are worshipers who come into the presence of Jesus to give glory to Him. Make sure that you maintain this focus.

✓ Keep learning yourself. Take dance classes and Bible studies to keep growing.

COSTUMING FROM SOUL TO SOLE

Modest, Artistic, Simple, Washable

What's the big deal? It's only a costume right? Nope. It's not just a costume. It's a major part of the presentation. In dance ministry, the costume choice is as important as the music and movement choices.

Costume mistakes can pull down the validity of a program. Don't get defensive about this issue. Just remember that dance ministry is visual. Listen to the leaders above you. Get wise and think through the following tips:

1. *Be more conservative in attire than you think is necessary.* There are people in the congregation who have not been exposed to the arts. As a leader, that should not make you afraid, but it should make you careful when you choose your costumes. Be artistic to the concept. Keep beauty in mind as one significant aspect because beauty helps people enter into worship and experience an important quality of God's character. Beauty is healing.

2. A costume can easily distract the congregation (especially men) if the garments are not loose. Don't be embarrassed to talk about the stuff that most people don't want to talk about. If a dancer has a large bust, kindly tell her that she needs to find a bra that "locks and loads" her bust (no dancing bustlines). Also, consider costume size. Men and women both have perceptions about the size of clothing they want to wear as opposed to their true size. In SonLight, we wear a size bigger than what we normally buy. I've also seen inappropriate undergarment colors. You can't wear a white dress with a black bra. And consider how a costume will appear with lighting effects. See Appendix J for a deeper look at costume choice.

3. Realize that color communicates meaning. Black is usually not the best choice for most dances. Your dancers might like it ("It makes me look skinny"). Black should be used to communicate dances dealing with Satan, death, evil, grief, etc. Purple, orange, blue, green, white, gold, silver, red, and pastels can all be used for a dance. Just make sure that your choice is conceptual to the song or text. Check with your church/ministry setting as to the decorative colors on site. Incorporate the two together if you can. Typically, the more modern the music style, the more pants (for the ladies) can be chosen. When dresses are preferable, listen for softer, lyrical song arrangements. Men, even professional dancers, are usually best in slacks (with a percentage of stretch material in the garment that you buy) during a church worship presentation.

4. Buy washable, no-iron fabrics that allow for ease of movement and ongoing use. Whether you sew your own costumes or order them, use materials that don't distract others from seeing the movement message of the song. Washable velvets, crepes, and synthetic fabrics are all good choices. If you are blessed to have a church budget to buy costumes, build up a costume closet that has colors and styles that will work in a variety of settings.

5. Don't make the mistake of waiting until the last minute to choose worship attire. Pray about costume choice as soon as you have a

new ministry project to consider. If you must order costumes or props (flags, ribbons, etc.), they usually take several weeks to arrive. If you order online, make an initial personal call to the company to see if the item(s) you need are in stock.

6. I've often used simplicity in style to guide my choices. As a rule, simplicity neutralizes costuming distractions so that on-lookers can focus on and worship Jesus during a presentation.

7. Don't get swayed by dancers who might be well-meaning but who may not really understand the reasons for the importance of ministry attire. "Let's wear this" or "that would look current" sometimes reflect self-serving reasons for costume choice. Consider the costume options that you have for each dance and listen to God's leading when you decide what to wear for ministry presentation.

8. Don't include costume discussion during a rehearsal as you will lose important rehearsal time and end up on a rabbit trail.

9. Let dancers know about costumes in your weekly email or text. I usually ask them to come to a particular rehearsal 15 minutes early or stay 15 minutes after rehearsal to try on costumes.

10. Wear the skirts or pants for the costume starting with the second or third gathering. Dancers will have the opportunity to get used to dancing with a skirt or pants that might trip them or come undone.

11. SonLight has clear plastic garment bags that each dancer uses to store his or her costume. After each rehearsal, they are placed on a clothing rack. I also tape a sheet of paper to the front of each bag for dancer and song identification (for use in numerous dances). The result? Garments don't disappear or get mixed up using this system. Email garment guidelines to dancers or talk about them in rehearsal.

Now on to the written standards I give to dancers:

Garment Guidelines for Ladies

- The worship attire worn by members of dance ministry is owned by _____Church. We have specific garment guidelines for its use.

- Please make sure your outfit fits in a modest way. If one garment fits tightly, and one garment is much larger, go with the larger one. Err on the side of looseness.

- Wear a tight fitting sports bra as an undergarment choice, particularly if your bra cup size exceeds an A cup. Bust line motion should not be a focus point at any time in SonLight. Gender differences dictate a special sensitivity to this issue. I have seen women involved in dramas and participating as worship singers on the stage who distract from an otherwise lovely presentation when they are not wise in undergarment choice. If you have a question in this area, please feel free to call me.

- Along with a sports bra, plan to wear either a white leotard with underarm pads or a white t-shirt with underarm pads for special protection of the worship garments during dress rehearsals and during the worship service. Most dancers sweat during dress rehearsals and in the worship services. When that occurs, we can wash our undergarments at home without ruining the outfit we are wearing. It's also really nice to inherit a garment that has been nicely taken care of rather than the alternative (Pads can be bought at any sewing store).

- Unless indicated, do not wear watches, earrings, or hair bows during presentations.

- Make sure the hair is tied back from the face so that when the movement is shown, hair or other distracting articles does not block facial expression.

- For most presentations, use long-sleeved attire and high-necked tops. Generally, long sleeved garments communicate modesty as people worship. Skirt or dress hems should fall below the knee. Always wear culottes under skirts or dresses.

- It is biblical to know that God designed the body and its beauty. We praise God for this special gift and are thankful for all sizes and shapes of women. Let us handle the beauty of the body delicately so that we glorify God and give all who watch us an offering worthy of the Lord.

"Do you not know that your bodies are temples of the Holy Spirit?"
(1 Corinthians 6:19).

"I urge you, brothers and sisters, in view of God's mercy, to offer your bodies as a living sacrifice, holy and pleasing to God—this is true and proper worship" (Romans 12:1).

Garment Guidelines for Men

- Please make sure that the shirt and pants that you have fit you loosely. If one top or pair of pants is slightly tight, and another choice is much larger, go with the larger one. Err on the side of looseness.

- Wear a white t-shirt (or another color if that is best) underneath the shirt for a particular presentation both for lighting purposes as well as for special protection of the garments during dress rehearsals and during the worship service. Most sweat during dress rehearsals and in the worship services. When that occurs, we can wash our undergarments at home without ruining the outfit we are wearing. It's also really nice to inherit a garment that has been nicely taken care of rather than the alternative. (Pads can be bought at any sewing store.)

- Unless indicated, do not wear watches or other noticeable jewelry during presentations.

- Make sure that hair or other distracting articles do not block facial expression.

- For most presentations, use long-sleeved attire and consider using regular men's slacks in ministry presentations.

"Do you not know that your bodies are temples of the Holy Spirit?" (1 Corinthians 6:19).

"I urge you, brothers and sisters, in view of God's mercy, to offer your bodies as a living sacrifice, holy and pleasing to God—this is true and proper worship" (Romans 12:1).

Final Dress/Tech

Final dress/tech rehearsal for 'Open Me'

- Make sure that the entrance and exits for the service/ministry presentation are smooth. I usually clarify this in rehearsals prior to presentation day. Otherwise, PIM looks ragged.

- Ask the worship pastor/ministry leader to have a run through of the dance with all technical elements prior to the start of a service/ministry presentation.

- Find out the exact time of presentation in a service/ministry setting. Fifteen minutes prior to PIM presentation, have dancers warm-up quietly so that they prepare their hearts before they actually present the dance. Talking about everyday activities just before dancers go onstage distract from organic worship. As mentioned previously, it's easy to turn a dance into a performance instead of a ministry presentation. Quiet worshipful hearts lead dancers into organic Spirit-led worship.

Dance Explanation in Service/Ministry Setting

Write an introduction to a prepared dance with the worship pastor/ministry leader prior to presentation. As God leads, share the explanation to the dance in written form (in the service folder), using audio and/or video recordings, or stated live whenever possible. An explanation edifies the congregation in faith, clarifies movement content, and ushers people into responsive worship.

Example:

This morning's dance presentation of "Belong" by Chris Rice captures a salvation message designed to breakdown cultural misunderstanding of the Gospel. The choreography shows the story of a man who discovers the gift of belonging to God and the wonder of fellowship in the King's family.

The woman in white represents the "seen and unseen" presence of the Holy Spirit with the other two dancers representing different life circumstances that God used to draw the man to Himself. By the end of the dance, these two dancers become the care and love that embody "Father Love" and "Brother Jesus." All three dancers demonstrate God's purposeful work of love in the life in a man who initially dismissed the Lordship of Jesus as irrelevant.

PRESENTATION DAY

Arrival

- Change into costume and gather together at a set arrival time.
- Pray for the dance group and include prayer for the service as well as for the Christians and non-Christians who attend.
- Quietly worship and pray as warm-ups occur.
- Run the dance in the rehearsal room.

- Remind dancers that if they have been faithful to rehearse one time per day and faithful in the rehearsal process, they need to give grace to themselves if mistakes occur during the presentation.

PASTORAL TRUST

Educate your pastor about the value of visual communication through dance and build trust as you show submission to him or her. When the pastor/ministry leader is hesitant or says 'no' to something you consider important, stop insisting on what you want and listen. Makes changes if you can. There will be a next time. You may not gain what you wanted for a specific dance, but, in the long run, you will earn trust by respecting leadership decisions. Next time he or she will tend to be more attentive to you because you have honored his or her viewpoint. And if nothing changes, and you are frustrated, remember that God is sovereign. He often uses these situations to test your motives and grow your character.

In the course of leading and choreographing for dance ministry, you will meet with a worship pastor or ministry leader to plan dance presentation possibilities. Come to the meeting prepared. If you know a service has a focused theme, take the time to pray and investigate songs or text that would strengthen the theme when presented in a dance. Write up a list of possibilities with songs that match future sermon/service/ministry dates. On the other hand, you might have a leader that doesn't want you to listen to songs ahead of time. He or she might hand you a song to consider. He or she might even tell you to do a certain song and not ask your opinion.

Work with the style of whomever God allows. That's how trust is built. Have a good attitude as you show love and support to ministry leaders or pastors and watch the dance ministry grow. Don't expect your viewpoint and your choices to lead the ultimate outcome of what takes place. Take responsibility for biblical responses no matter how you feel (1 Peter 2:2).

THE FOUR MAIN REHEARSAL ESSENTIALS

Let's summarize the four major essentials from this chapter (after knowing God, listening to God, and loving God and others). I would encourage you to look in Chapter 6 to review the four essentials from a pastoral perspective:

1. Target your choreography.

2. Preview.

3. Dress considerations.

4. Educate others.

Target Your Choreography (i.e. "Have a Point")

-   Create choreography that communicates a biblical concept.

-   Identify your choreography target prior to starting choreography. Don't assume that you know it; otherwise, you will often default and diverge into "movement stuff."

-   Prepare carefully before rehearsals begin.

Preview

-   Set up committee members to preview the dance before it is presented.

-   Send out the preview letter using the criteria explained earlier.

-   Give a preview sheet for each reviewer to fill out and turn in. Have at least two people preview the dance. File preview sheets to keep for future reference.

-   Not only does this structure keep dance accountable to communicate the identified target, but it is also protective of dancers and choreographers. As with all church staff, there will be individuals who criticize the arts (even when they communicate well). When a dance has been previewed, a dance ministry has other strong voices to affirm it.

Dress

-   Dress with modest garments and make movement choices that glorify God and allow for worship at the same time.

- Consult this chapter and Appendix J for garment guidelines and costume choices.

- Do not include choreography choices that are inappropriately erotic in nature.

Education

- Educate pastoral staff and the congregation about dance ministry

- Choose to be submissive to the leadership perspective above you.

- Win trust by listening to them and meeting their objectives. Don't argue to win.

- Slowly coach them to your point of view.

- If the doors for dance ministry are closed, pray and be content. But continue to pray. "Making it happen" disallows trust in a sovereign God and will suck you into carnal reaction and anger instead of godly response. Hold dance ministry loosely. Don't let it become an idol framed by your ego.

REHEARSAL RUBRIC

I use the rubric to help me or another choreographer to see how they are doing with appropriate goals as a dance rehearses. Remember, if the rehearsal structure is not crafted with biblical goals, it easily dissolves into a carnal gathering with carnal goals such as eating, texting, whining, and gossiping. Don't allow that to happen in your program. Turn this evaluation into your pastor or ministry leader at the end of rehearsals on a particular dance or evaluate yourself during the course of each rehearsal. You can also use this format to help new choreographers as they lead dancers in dance ministry for the first time. Grow in faith as you lead dance ministry. Enjoy the process!

"For Christians, artistic experiences can foster right responses to God. For one thing, the arts have always been a part of worship. The Bible itself is artistic."[61]

Look below to place dates of rehearsals in the boxes as indicated; check other boxes if this element has occurred during a rehearsal, and then comment as it is needed for needed areas of improvement.

---

[61] Ryken, 266.

Rehearsal Rubric for evaluation of choreographers; place dates of rehearsals in box below; check other boxes if this element has occurred during a rehearsal and then comment as it is needed for needed areas of improvement.

Rehears al	Date	Start/ Stop On Time	Prayer	Conceptu al Ice Breaker	Warm-Ups/ Worship	Clear Commu n-ication/ Weekly Emails	Teaching/ Clarity of Choreogr -aphy	Costume Prepar-ation	Intentional Choreo-graphy/ Mention of Concept
1									
Comments:									
2									
Comments:									
3									
Comments:									
4									
Comments:									
5									
Comments:									
6									
Comments:									
7									
Comments:									
8									
Comments:									

Mary M. Bawden

Chapter 6

Soul or Sole? Problems for Pastors

Final Presentation of 'Give Me Your Eyes' incorporating set and props

"Even with a strong biblical basis for the use of sacred dance, historically, we will see that there have always been those who were afraid to use the gift of dance. In every area of congregational life, we find those who do not have the spiritual discernment and maturity to separate the sacred from the profane. Rather than allow fear to keep us from God's good gifts, we must learn to use them appropriately."[62]

---

[62] Taken from *Dancing for Joy* by Murray Silberling. Copyright © 1995. All rights reserved. Used by

permissions of Messianic Jewish Publishers, 6120 Day Long Lane, Clarksville, MD 21029.

www.messianicjewish.net.

Dear pastor/ministry leader,

Can you imagine serving a meal without the correct ingredients? Or ignoring a recipe's directions? To make a successful meal, one needs to combine the right ingredients, practical methods, and creative presentation. And that—voila—applies to dance ministry too.

First, thank you for reading this chapter about the gift of dance. Dancers want prayer-in-motion to be part of the recipes used for the proclamation of the gospel. As dance ministry leaders and participants, we pray for Spirit-led dances to transform hearts as congregants hear about the Bread of Life. And we are blessed to have pastoral support when we glorify God with movement recipes that visualize embodied faith.

Dancers know that we present several challenges for you. Most of you don't have a dance background and don't relate to an art form that is foreign to you. Even if movement pulls at your heart, it's not easy for you to shop for the right ingredients. And there are other elements you question. That's why I have written this book. It captures both theory and practical structure to blend successful dance communication and ministry into the right menu for church worship.

I encourage you to read Chapter 1 to understand the foundation for dance ministry. In a nutshell, the recipe for Spirit-led dance ministry involves choreography that identifies a biblical concept. Then we communicate God's heart to a congregation through the strength of sensory, non-verbal movement language. This is prayer-in-motion.

In the dance world and in the church world, understanding the language of movement clarifies the difference between dance, Christian dance, and prayer-in-motion. Without that knowledge, many dancers and many pastors or ministry leaders don't know how to mix the right ingredients for the gift of dance in the church.

The rest of this chapter consists of several practical recipes to start a dance ministry in your church or ministry setting. I have also included additional guidelines in the appendix section. If you read these, they will help you understand how a non-dance person can know how to oversee a successful dance ministry.

Last but not least, this chapter includes comments from a worship pastor with whom I have worked for more than 10 years. His insightful, faith-based support has been invaluable to me, as he has seen prayer-in-motion unfold. It is my hope that you will use the ingredients in this book to communicate the gospel from soul to sole using the art of dance.

Let's get started with the four main essentials (a.k.a. ingredients) for a successful Christian dance ministry. Each essential includes practical tools for implementation.

CREATING AND IMPLEMENTING A SPIRIT-LED CHRISTIAN DANCE MINISTRY

Essential 1: Targeted Choreography (Chapters 1 & 4)

- You should plan to meet with a choreographer to choose a dance song or text that glorifies God within the framework of a Sunday worship service or ministry setting and choose a date for presentation at least eight weeks in advance. Remember, dance ministry not only rehearses movement but creates movement. Give us the time we need to present a God honoring dance.

- Just as you have ministry goals, you can expect that a ministry dance will have an identified biblical concept in the song or text choice and in the choreography creation.

- The movement you see will not pantomime the words in the song (Don't look for literal translation of a concept in dance choreography. The gospel movement will access the heart through sensory, visual communication as opposed to intellectual arguments). Remember that dance is its own language. However, by the end of the dance, the sum total of all of the movements should partner with the words of the song or text to "see" one identified biblical concept through the choreography.

- Each identified conceptual dance will fall within at least one of the following worship categories: praise; beauty (healing and restoration); teaching (truth, story, or symbol); celebration; and/or prayer.

Practical Help: A choreographer will identify the choreography target and song choice in the meeting with you prior to the start of rehearsals.

That choreography target will also be written down when the choreography/leadership covenant is signed.

Essential 2: Leadership Criteria and Signed Choreography/Leadership Covenant (Chapter 2)

A dance ministry leader/choreographer is a dancer who:

- Has a personal relationship with the Lord Jesus.

- Views Scripture as revealed transcendent truth and enjoys studying and reading the Bible.

- Has a desire to choreograph based on the leading of the Holy Spirit.

- Is submissive to decisions made by church staff.

- Desires to be held to preview standards in choice of music, costuming, and choreography.

- Is in agreement with the leadership/choreography covenant.

Prior to each dance, you can expect the choreographer to sign a leadership/choreography covenant with you. If you use two different people to fill each of these tasks, meet together with both people and sign a covenant with each one. You can also expect to be copied with dance ministry emails/texts during the process of a dance so that you are in the communication loop as a dance progresses.

Practical Help: The leadership/choreography covenant is below. This covenant is between the leader/choreographer of the dance ministry and you. It is also found in Appendix D. You might also be interested to look at the rehearsal covenant listed in Appendix G (the covenant between the dancers and the leader/ choreographer). The success of a dance and dance ministry rests with the choices made by the leader/choreographer of the dance ministry.

Leadership/Choreography Covenant

I wish to participate at _____Church/Ministry using my gifts as a leader and/or choreographer, honoring the Lord Jesus through prayer-in-motion. With grace as the foundation, I agree to the following:

A. All of the conditions listed in the dance ministry member covenant used for the preparation of any prayer-in-motion (See Chapter 5).

B. I want to grow in my personal relationship with Jesus. Because of that, I will spend daily time knowing God, listening to God, and loving God and others. List the personal Bible study you are involved in: _____.

C. I commit to be transparent if any disagreements should occur within the context of movement preparation and I commit to speak directly to the person(s) involved. I will use electronic or personal communication with the ministry supervisor regarding any incidents. A decision not to gossip with others will be the philosophical foundation of all interaction.

D. I commit to display an attitude of submission to the leaders above me—whether in agreement with those decisions or not—as well as accountability in reference to choreography, music, and costuming choices.

E. I commit to the study of the biblical concept being choreographed.

F. I resolve to have the integrity to complete any individual project responsibilities agreed upon and to follow through with administrative communication (using a cc format in emails) and completion of the dance/rehearsal process. Active membership at _____ Church.

G. I commit to my attendance as leader/choreographer (and attendance of individual choreographers if a program rotates choreographers) at pastoral planning meetings.

H. I commit to consistent meetings (as requested) with _____ regarding growth in faith and Bible study, personal interactions with dancers, and the choreography process.

Date: _____ Signature of leader: _____

Name of motion prayer:

Biblical concept targeted for choreography:

Essential 3: Modest Garment and Movement Choices (Chapters 3 & 5)
(See Appendix J for a deeper look at costume choice).

- You should expect modesty, beauty, and/or conceptual intent from costumes.

- You can expect the choreography will not have erotic movements.

- Feel free to comment directly to the choreographer if the costumes are not modest or the movement is inappropriate.

- Plan your yearly budget with dance ministry costs (costumes, equipment, and sets).

Practical Help: Garment Guidelines

Ladies: Because the worship attire worn by members of this dance ministry is owned by _____Church, we have specific garment guidelines for its use.

1. Please make sure the outfit fits you in a modest way. If one garment fits tightly, and one garment is much larger, go with the larger one. Err on the side of looseness.

2. Wear a tight-fitting sports bra as an undergarment choice, particularly if your bra cup size exceeds an A cup. Bust-line motion should not be a focus point at any time in dance ministry. Gender differences dictate a special sensitivity to this issue. I have seen women involved in dramas and on the stage as singers who distract from an otherwise lovely presentation when they are not wise in undergarment choice. If you have a question in this area, please feel free to call the dance ministry leader.

3. Along with a sports bra, plan to wear either a white leotard with underarm pads or a white t-shirt with underarm pads for special protection of the worship garments during dress rehearsals and during the worship service. Most sweat during dress rehearsals and in the worship services. When that occurs, we can wash our undergarments at home without ruining the outfit we are wearing.

It's also really nice to inherit a garment that has been nicely taken care of rather than the alternative. (Pads can be bought at any sewing store.)

4. Unless indicated, do not wear watches, earrings, or hair bows during presentations.

5. Make sure the hair is tied back from the face so that when the movement is shown, facial expression is not blocked by hair or other distracting articles.

6. For most presentations, use long-sleeved attire and high-necked tops; generally, long sleeved garments communicate modesty as people worship. Skirt or dress hems should fall below the knee. Always use culottes under skirts or dresses.

7. Remember, it is biblical to know that God designed the body and its beauty. We praise God for this special gift and are thankful for all sizes and shapes of women. Let us handle the beauty of the body delicately so that we glorify God and give all who watch us an offering worthy of the Lord.

"Do you not know that your bodies are temples of the Holy Spirit?" (1 Corinthians 6:19).

"I urge you, brothers and sisters, in view of God's mercy, to offer your bodies as a living sacrifice, holy and pleasing to God—this is true and proper worship" (Romans 12:1).

Men: Because the worship attire worn by members of this dance ministry is owned by _____Church, we have specific garment guidelines for its use.

1. Please make sure that the shirt and pants you wear fit loosely. If one top or pants at home is slightly tight, and another choice is much larger, go with the larger one. Err on the side of looseness.

2. Wear a white t-shirt (or another color if that is best) underneath the shirt for a particular presentation both for lighting purposes as well

as for special protection of the garments during dress rehearsals and during the worship service. Most sweat during dress rehearsals and in the worship services. When that occurs, we can wash our undergarments at home without ruining the outfit we are wearing. It's also really nice to inherit a garment that has been nicely taken care of rather than the alternative. (Pads can be bought at any sewing store.)

3. Unless indicated, do not wear watches or other noticeable jewelry during presentations.

4. Make sure that hair or other distracting articles do not block facial expression.

5. For most presentations, use long-sleeved attire and consider using regular men's slacks in ministry presentations.

"Do you not know that your bodies are temples of the Holy Spirit?" (1 Corinthians 6:19).

"I urge you, brothers and sisters, in view of God's mercy, to offer your bodies as a living sacrifice, holy and pleasing to God—this is true and proper worship" (Romans 12:1).

Essential 4 Dance Preview (Chapter 5)

Preview committee for 'Architecture' a dance presented in the fall of 2014(former director of children's ministries Jeanie Osterberg and former elder Henry Meinders) discuss what they observed in the choreography and song with the cast

- The choreographer should contact you prior to the presentation of a scheduled dance so that you can either come to one of the last rehearsals or see a video of the dance.

- The choreographer will also need your help to set up a preview committee, composed of elders and church leaders, to see the dance prior to presentation. Two to three members of this committee, not the entire committee, should see each dance before it is presented to the congregation.

- You or your church secretary should contact volunteers to preview the dance on a rehearsal date already scheduled.

- The choreographer should have preview sheets available to fill out at preview rehearsals.

- Each volunteer should fill out a preview sheet and turn it in to the choreographer for the dance. The choreographer should keep these sheets on file and be prepared to share them as requested by you or other interested church members.

- Dance ministry preview should occur before the final rehearsal of a dance so that committee concerns can be addressed if needed.

- You can expect a good attitude from the choreographer if you or the preview committee does not feel the dance communicates biblically and/or if the presentation is cancelled. For success, look for scores consistently above five (10 being the highest score).

Practical Help for Preview:
Sample invitation letter to send to preview committee:

Dear --------,

Greetings in the name of the Lord! I am honored to write you this letter, and I do so on behalf of SonLight prayer-in-motion at Trinity Church. SonLight is a ministry of the arts that uses movement as a non-verbal tool to share the Gospel of Jesus Christ through the faith of those involved in a particular dance. Part of God's direction for this ministry has been to ask men and women of faith to come into the rehearsal process to view the motion prayer before it is presented to the congregation.

Each dance that you see is purposefully chosen and prayerfully considered prior to rehearsal. I hope that you have been blessed by this ministry. However, I believe that to maintain God's standards and not my own, SonLight is called to invite mature Christ-followers into the rehearsal process to make sure that dance speaks biblically into the hearts of those watching.

I would love to have you on the list of those Christ-followers willing to serve in this capacity. This would involve the following:

1. *To read Chapter 1 from Soul to Sole Choreography. That chapter defines the philosophy and goals of prayer-in-motion for the dance ministry at this church. Note that each dance should communicate a biblical concept.*

2. *To come to one of the last rehearsals of a dance and view the dance to see if it succeeds as a ministry tool leading believers and non-believers to be drawn to the Lord Jesus.*

3. *To give honest feedback to the choreographer as well as the group involved in the movement. Ephesians 4:15 asks believers to be "speaking the truth in love."*

4. *To fill out a dance preview form.*

5. *No movement skills or background is necessary; FAITH is the critical factor.*

6. *If you choose to place yourself on this list, the person setting up your involvement might call you one or two times a year. If you cannot come to a rehearsal, all you have to do is say no.*

7. *Call _____ to let me know of your involvement.*

8. *If you have any questions or concerns, feel free to give me a personal call.*

9. *As God leads you, pray for the motion prayer you have viewed.*

Thank you for considering this very special involvement in dance ministry.
much love, Mary.

For you: "And whatever you do, whether in word or deed, do it all in the name of the Lord Jesus, giving thanks to God the Father through him" (Colossians 3:17).

Evaluation Form for Dance Preview (see Appendix H)

Name of previewer:_____

Name of dance:_____

Date: _____

Write out the biblical concept that the movement and words in the song or text communicate:

Evaluate: (1 Low; 10 High)   Rate (1 Low;10 High) Comments

	Rate (1 Low;10 High)	Comments
Overall response to dance		
Communication of biblical Concept		
Technical level clean & clear		
Costumes		
Music		
Unaddressed problems?		
Worship of dancers		

"Through worship is clearly an embodied, multisensory experience, what is significant in worship is that all of this sensory experience contributes to a perception of the beauty, love, and grace of the Triune God."[63]

I hope you now know and understand the four essentials to begin a dance ministry. You don't need a dance background to implement dance in your church or ministry setting. And remember, the responsibility for successful choreography communication rests with the choreographer/leader. Simply follow the steps for success and the power of dance will flavor how you share the gospel. That is the goal.

SOUL TO SOLE TIPS ABOUT DANCERS FOR PASTOR/MINISTRY LEADERS

Dancers want to use their gifts to promote the gospel. They are especially excited to live in a visual age that needs visual communication. Remember the strength of non-verbal communication. Only 7 percent of communication rests with words by themselves. "Active, interdisciplinary, and sensory-teaching approaches use a greater array of human intelligence, promote deeper understanding and better retention, and inspire an inner desire to learn."[64]

We need honesty as you communicate with us. We also need the freedom to be honest with you. Don't be upset if we disagree with you. On the other hand, we will support your final decisions because we understand submission to you.

We need a separate room for rehearsal. Of course, when we aren't using this room, it can accommodate many other groups. If it is possible, we need mirrors installed on one wall. We use them to correct and adjust movement. By the second or third rehearsal, we need to finish each rehearsal in the space used for ministry presentation. We will also need to use tape on the floor for spacing as needed.

---

[63] John D. Witvliet, "The Worship: How Can Art Serve the Corporate Worship of the Church?" in *For the Beauty of the Church*, ed. W. David O. Taylor (Grand Rapids, MI: Baker Books, 2010), 61. Fair use.

[64] A. K. Kanter, "Arts in Our Schools: Arts based school reform that applies the concept of interdisciplinary study and active learning to teach to the multiple intelligences" (unpublished master's thesis, University of Northern Colorado, Greely, 1993).

We inherit all kinds of floors for rehearsal and ministry, but a wood floor is the best thing for our feet when we dance. We can get injured by dancing consistently on concrete covered by carpet. Please consider this option when you build a new room or when flooring needs to be replaced.

Don't hesitate to include a brief explanation of a dance in the church bulletin or in remarks that you make before its presentation. Although the movement communication is defined with an identified worship category and conceptual choreography target, some people in the congregation will not understand the non-verbal language of dance. Christendom is filled with people who are uncomfortable with dance as well as uncomfortable with the use of their body. They are helped with an interpreter for this unknown language. I would encourage you to educate your congregation as to the value of arts that give glory to God. Release them to respond to worship with simple movement and watch them grow in faith.

We need men to participate in prayer-in-motion. Otherwise, we won't present a full visual picture of the gospel. Songs that invite male participation depend on the style of music and the message involved (See Chapters 4 and 5). Help your choreographer to identify strong men of faith for dance ministry involvement. Assure these men that they will not be given feminine movements that will undermine their God-given strength and leadership. Your support will be important. Feel free to show them SonLight videos that have used men in the past and look in Chapter 3 to find out about a movement tool called "genesis." That tool will access their movement base in a non-threatening way.

When you meet with a choreographer, let him or her know if you want researched songs on a particular theme before the meeting. Some of you will like help with musical selection and some of you will prefer to do song research by yourself. Whatever you choose is fine. Just make sure that you communicate your expectations clearly.

TRAINED AND UNTRAINED (CONGREGATIONAL) DANCERS

Nationally and internationally, there is a wide range of Christ-followers called into dance ministry, with a wide variety of dance backgrounds.

How do we decide who is best prepared to carry on dance ministry? Are the trained dancers in a better position to serve the Church because they move with a stronger technical base? Do they speak with movement language that is more powerful and more beautiful because of their structured technique? On the other hand, does formal training squeeze spontaneity out of dance presentations? Do untrained dancers have more freedom in worship and faith because of their organic movement base, or is this untrained base too awkward to use? Finally, should age restrict movement participation in ministry? In the secular world, dancers have a short life. Does the same philosophy hold true for those who dance in church settings?

The Scripture reveals a God who loves and enfolds His people with movement. The incarnation of Jesus is a study of God's movement to humanity—a redemptive dance for all. Dance in the church needs to reflect the same kind of enfolding approach. This is because the physical technique of everyone considered "untrained" is actually refined and "trained" in a different way than those who take formal classes. Dance is different from other artistic forms that require skill. It takes months of practice to learn to master the violin. It takes years of practice to sculpt art. However, everyone has the mastery of refined physical technique because the class occurs everyday. The challenge begins with the assumption that dance training only occurs with formal dance classes. The reality is that the body begins to build an accessible and complete technical base from birth. This technical foundation needs to be recognized and then shaped according to movement intent. Dance ministry uses the body to give glory to God through worship with power and purpose. It doesn't matter whether the movement is simple or if it involves professionally trained ballerinas with complex technique. What defines its success should be the clarity of movement communication. That is why Christendom should welcome both trained and untrained dancers (or congregational dancers) as part of a wonderful family. Neither trained nor untrained dancers should be penalized for what they have, or do not have. Rather, both groups share a common resource to help those inside and outside the church to see an embodied faith.

S. B. Savage once wrote, "Dance can bring back more of ourselves with which to know Christ, and, in a sense, can bring back to us more of

Christ."[65] Enfolding believers with formal training, as well as those who have never taken technical dance classes, can facilitate a wider umbrella for dance ministry that communicates the gospel. All ages, training, and genders should develop choreography based from the movement level that they have when they participate in dance ministry. In the best of circumstances, organic dance expression from the choreographer and from the dancers should develop worship movement from the inside out as a visible manifestation of personal inner faith. When believers and secular on-lookers see both trained and untrained dancers moving with biblical content, choreography with meaning internalizes transcendent truth.

> *"The purpose of bringing form to embodiment . . . is to recognize and live out the truth that form does inform the text and us kinesthetically."[66]*

The non-verbal language of dance speaks through a physical, technical foundation that everyone has, everyone can use, and everyone can relate to. Different people will favor different elements of the dance presentations—both from trained and untrained dancers. However, both groups of dancers should have a Spirit-led call to dance, be well-rehearsed, communicate biblical truth through worship and give glory to God. The result presents a faith that is visual, practical, and open to all who are called.

"But whoever lives by the truth comes into the light, so that it may be seen plainly that what they have done has been done in the sight of God" (John 3:21).

"Dance is the hidden language of the soul." Martha Graham

---

[65] Savage, 74.

[66] P. A. Moeller, *A Kinesthetic Homiletic—Embodying Gospel in Preaching* (Minneapolis: Fortress Press, 1993), 89.

SOUL TO SOLE DANCE FORMS FOR CORPORATE WORSHIP

There are three kinds of dance forms for corporate worship using either trained or untrained dancers. They are seen in the following ways:

1. As spontaneous acts of worship to a particular song or event done by either a dance group or by individual congregational members.

2. As prepared, choreographed presentations that the congregation watches.

3. As congregational movement prayers led by a leader, who invites the congregation to worship Jesus through simple corporate movements.

Spontaneous Worship (aka Prophetic Dance)

Although they are not rehearsed, spontaneous worship movements usually enhance a church service. Depending on the time, the sensitivity of the individual or individuals, and the context of ministry, there are occasions where this style of movement is beautifully used in a formal worship setting even though there has been no formal choreography or rehearsal time. Sometimes dance ministry groups use structured dance improvisation if a situation calls for it. However, the use of spontaneous dance in a worship service or ministry setting develops from the philosophy of the pastoral staff and the church setting.

Planned Worship

Prayer-in-motion (PIM) is purposefully designed for viewing by the Body of Christ (most of this book is a reference for movement prayers that are planned PIM dance ministry). While this kind of motion prayer is rehearsed, the Spirit-led rehearsal and presentation need to focus on embodied worship that gives glory to God. The goal for every dance should be to express faith to Jesus from soul to sole while communicating biblical concepts in the language of dance. Dances should not include mechanical movements that come across to those watching as a "technical performance" or unidentified feelings of movement stuff.

"The issue of spontaneous versus planned worship seems to cause people to take sides over which is more spiritual. Scripture gives us examples of each."[67]

Congregational Movement Prayers

Simple corporate motion prayers achieve holistic worship with unity and praise. A motion prayer occurs when a movement leader teaches a congregational movement prayer using three or four simple motions integrating the body, the mind, and the spirit as congregants follow. The leader invites (not forces) the congregation to move in faith and worship with him or her. Congregational motion in worship also mirrors the goal that exhorts a believer to live with an attitude of lifestyle worship. When all parts of a person bow before Christ in transcendent truth, the potential for personal transformation increases.

"Once a congregation's imagination gets into the act, literally, they become part of the experience, and this experience becomes internalized as part of their own make up. A lesson internalized is a lesson learned."[68]

A WORSHIP PASTOR'S PERSPECTIVE (by Worship Pastor Bill Born)

I have had the privilege of being the worship pastor for Trinity Church in Redlands, California since 2001. When I took over the role of worship pastor, I inherited a healthy worshiping congregation and a philosophy of worship ministry that included the arts as a needed and necessary component to our worship services. Dance was a thriving and prolific aspect of that ministry.

Our church exists in a community that values the arts. We have a handful of year-round community theater programs, strong music and theater programs at our schools, and a free outdoor summer music festival that draws thousands of people for its weekly Thursday and

---

[67] Noland, 24.

[68] Linda M. Goens, *Praising God Through the Lively Arts*, (Nashville: Abingdon Press, 1999), 13. Fair use.

Friday night programs. Our church is made up of people from our community.

I see myself as a typical worship leader, more musically inclined. I would not classify myself as an "artsy" person. But I courageously stepped into the worship pastor role and was fairly sure I could hang with the artists. I was in for a crash course in learning how to value, support, utilize, and—yes—defend the purpose of dance in the worship service; and more important, learn to love and shepherd the artists in our congregation.

Whether you are a choreographer, a dancer, a worship leader or pastor, or even someone who doesn't really get art at all, I hope you will see the value of dance as worship unto the Lord, appropriate in the corporate worship context, and a necessary part of building up the body of Christ, the Church.

Philosophy of Ministry

Dance ministry cannot thrive, let alone exist in the church if it doesn't fit within an accepted philosophy amongst church leadership and congregants. Our belief at Trinity Church is that God has equipped the people in our congregation with gifts, given by the Holy Spirit for the purpose of edifying the church. This is both true of those who are currently part of our church family and those who have yet to come to Christ. Those of us in pastoral and lay leadership strive to help people engage in using their gifts to glorify God and edify the church.

But here is something very important that I have discovered: Dance is not a spiritual gift. Neither is music, nor is a technical ability. These are not listed among the spiritual gifts in the Scripture.[69] Rather, dance is a God-given talent or ability through which God can and should be glorified.

The beauty of a dance is the heart of the dancer set on glorifying God. I see it in their faces. I see it in their choreography. That is where dance becomes worship. Glorifying God should happen in and out of the worship service, both when the church gathers together to worship and

---

[69] Romans 12, 1 Corinthians 12, Ephesians 4, and 1 Peter 4 list these gifts and clearly teach that "a manifestation of the Spirit is given to *all* believers."

goes out into the world to live for Christ. Dancers choreograph, rehearse, and then perform their piece as a "work of service, so that the body of Christ may be built up." This passage is the foundation of my philosophy of ministry:

> *"So Christ himself gave the apostles, the prophets, the evangelists, and the pastors and teachers, to equip his people for works of service, so that the body of Christ may be built up until we all reach unity in the faith and in the knowledge of the Son of God and become mature, attaining to the whole measure of the fullness of Christ" (Ephesians 4:11-13).*

As a pastor, I see my role clearly as to prepare God's people for the work of service so that the Body of Christ may be built up. This picture of building up the Body of Christ applies to both believers and non-believers.

Let's think about non-believers for a moment. You must join the body of Christ before you can be built up into it. The brick must first be added to the building, so to speak.

Christian dancers in the public square have a difficult role, but the light of Christ shines through brightly in the midst of a permeating darkness in the secular arena of the arts. If you are a professional dancer, or striving to be one, I want to encourage you. The Lord calls you His ambassador for the gospel and you do so by sharing the message: "Be reconciled to God!" (2 Corinthians 5:20). There is such potential there to minister on a personal level. It excites me to think of those who are far away being brought near, those who are in darkness being transferred into the marvelous light, and those, who feel valued only according to their performance, finding value simply and completely as a beloved child of God! Learning to perform, not for acceptance, but to bring praise to Him! God loves dancers; and they are a critical part of the Body of Christ.

Now let's think about the main context of the Ephesians 4 passage, the building up of believers. As previously stated, my role as a pastor is to prepare God's people (dancers) for service. When appropriate, these works of service take the form of dances in the worship service because that is the only place and time when the entire congregation meets together. In that context, the dancers are also on the giving end, exercising their spiritual gift through the means of dance. Considering the spiritual gifts listed in Scripture, we have dancers who are evangelistic and dancers who have the gift of teaching. We have dancers with the gift of faith, who should use that to encourage other believers' faith. There are dancers with the gift of helps and encouragement. Even healing can come as the heart is accessed, opening door to the transforming work of the Holy Spirit through the artistic display or telling of the message of Christ and the gospel. What comes before and after the dance in the worship service, or a written artist statement that accompanies the dance, are effective ways to enable dancers to use these gifts. Yet for the dancer, the choreography is the main avenue of communication.

When leading a group of dancers, the choreographer to some extent has the gift of administration as mentioned in 1 Corinthians 12:28. It takes quite an administrator to bring together a handful of very unique and peculiar artistic types. (I say that with deep affection, appreciation, and admission that I'm probably more "artsy" than I like to admit.) Of course, some of the gifts of the Spirit are spontaneous, and there is a time and a place for that too. The spontaneous spiritual gifts like tongues, working of miracles, and prophecy obviously thrive in the more charismatic traditions.

In conclusion, my philosophy of ministry gives me two points of action when it comes to those dances in our congregation who are dancers. First is to recognize and treat them as valuable members of our church family, there to be built up and to build up. Second is that my main work as a worship pastor is to prepare believers (dancers) for their works of service and then give them opportunities to serve, when appropriate, in the worship gatherings of God's people.

Should All Dance?

I have wrestled with this question from the beginning of my pastoral career. My answer is a qualified, yes. There is no doubt that Scripture qualifies dance as a form of worship, with our main proponent, not a woman, but a man, perhaps the manliest of all men in Scripture apart from Christ. A courageous warrior and a great leader, King David was also a musician, poet, and dancer—a worshiper of the Almighty God.

Second Samuel 6:14 says, "Wearing a linen ephod, David was dancing before the LORD with all his might." However, Scripture doesn't require dancing in the same way it commands us to sing. Psalm 149, for instance, commands us to sing to the Lord when we assemble together in worship, but the encouragement that follows is to "let them praise his name with dancing and make music to him with timbrel and harp" (Psalm 149:3). It seems like dancing and the use of musical instruments is naturally expected to accompany our songs of praise.

Whether or not we are "gifted" with movement, God created us to dance to physically express our joy and to that end, I think all should dance, young and old. Of course, we're all wired differently so some people's dancing might be a reserved sway while another would be more unrestrained. Either way, it is simply wonderful and certainly glorifying to our God of hope who fills us with all joy and peace as we trust in Him!

Scheduling Dances into the Worship Service

I must have a close working relationship with my choreographers and dance ministry leader in order to decide together what pieces are appropriate for the worship service.

Mary has outlined her criteria, which helps her to bring ideas to me that are already strong candidates. When we get together to decide on a piece, I process things with the general purpose of the worship service as a foundation. The main purpose of the worship service is two-fold: to glorify God as we worship Him and to edify and build up the church. All elements scheduled into the worship service should do both. Glorifying God is primarily a heart issue and so depends on the heart motivations of the dancer. Edifying the Body (congregation) so that they will be built up is the harder issue to address. My goal is to choose pieces that will access people's hearts.

For instance our dance ministry performed "Like Incense/Sometimes by Step" to encourage God's people to value His Word, declaring together, "O God, you are my God and I will ever praise you!" During the lengthy and powerful instrumental bridge of this song, someone read continuous verses from Psalm 119 leading us in prayerful meditation.

"I Love You, Lord" used simple body shapes to accompany this beautiful and well-known prayer to the Lord.

"Breath of Heaven" at Christmas gave an opportunity to enter into the story, just a solo voice and solo dancer taking us deep into the worshiping heart of Mary, the mother of our Lord.

"Your Great Name" at Easter identifies the power of believing in the name of the Lord, the marvelous things that happen to us when we confess His name, and of course, gives opportunity to sing out the name of Jesus. We had both the unbeliever and the believer in mind when we chose this piece, giving them both the opportunity to join in and confess Jesus as Lord.

Then "Please Be My Strength," another heart stirring prayer to accompany the closing, "Looking Back" theme of our final sermon of our Joseph series. Some of these dances are more reflective, some more celebratory, and some prayerful. Some are participatory, and others are slightly targeted toward the unbeliever who is watching and listening. All of them have elements of both participation and observation because quite frankly, that reflects the attitude of those in the congregation. The Spirit is moving in the lives of non-believers and believers, and we don't have full view of what He's doing. We must simply reflect what He's doing in our hearts and trust that He's doing similar things in others.

Once we choose a piece, we must decide how it fits in the flow of the service. The congregation finds it easy to relate to a celebratory dance. It is the most natural use of dance, so I think it should be the most widely used in the worship service. We like to use these early on in the service and sometimes to close our services. Often we add dance as a worship expression to a song that is already well known and loved by our congregation. However, we must not limit dance to just celebration. We often place prayerful dances right in the midst of our worship time, or often as the climax to a set of worship songs. The most challenging aspect for us has been to schedule a dance either just before or in response to the sermon. This must be done in close partnership with the preaching pastor. Our pastor doesn't plan his opening sermon illustration or closing application until he has studied the Bible passage in depth. These are the last decisions he makes, intentionally seeking to hear from the Lord through His Word and not insert his own agenda into the preaching or teaching. While frustrating for us who need to plan ahead, I now see this as a huge positive—honoring the Lord through the faithful teaching of His Word. There are plenty of other places to incorporate dance into the worship service, so we focus on those times and occasionally find a perfect fit on either side of the sermon.

The Worship Pastor and His Colleagues

Our senior pastor supports the use of the arts in the worship service. This is a huge blessing to my worship planning team.[70] We both agree that the artistic elements are not the central focus, but he stands behind me in supporting their appropriate use.

I have learned first of all to apply the "no surprises" rule. This applies to all programming, especially when something is out of the ordinary or may be controversial. Anytime we schedule an artistic element either side of his message, I let him know about it, making sure that he is okay with it and prepared to take or give the handoff. I seek his input into the content and placement. Since he is in authority as my leader, he has complete veto rights to move or remove something within or from the service. Good decisions and proper communication early on in the creative process stop this from happening too late in the game, which is very hard on the dancers who have prepared and invested in the piece.

Trust your intuition and take any ideas to your senior pastor right away for approval or input. This takes great flexibility and humility on the part of both the worship pastor and his dance team leader. We must hold loosely to our artistic ideas and plans and encourage the artists we lead to do the same.

Second, I have a review system with my senior pastor. Each element of the worship service can be viewed as positive, neutral, or negative in its impact toward achieving the purpose of the worship service (outlined above as glorifying God, building/edifying the people). We try to view this not just individually, but together, sensing the general perspective of our church family gathered in the worship service. Our goal is never to have a negative, to allow for some neutral, but always to shoot for

---

[70] I partner with a volunteer team of both artists and technicians who help me plan, execute, and review the worship services at Trinity. Each member leads his or her own team of volunteers. We meet every other week in each other's homes for a two-hour meeting. We oversee dance, drama, music, film, faith stories, art and décor, lighting, sound, media, and stage management. We have fun!

positive. Positive elements, dances in this context, not only have great content, but they also are well executed technically and have been placed well in the worship service.

One dance recently performed was a neutral in both of our minds. While the choreography and artistry of the dancers was exceptional, I failed on my end in our transition into the dance. Transitions are so important! Taking too long to set up made it feel more like a performance piece than a natural response to the message. A disorganized entry of worship singers was distracting right at the climax of the piece. Also, we failed to invite the congregation to participate. Praise be to God that He works within and regardless of our weakness and failures. I'm sure the Lord was glorified and many people were edified anyway. All is not lost when a dance piece is a neutral and when we learn from our mistakes.

The congregation certainly doesn't expect perfection either. Even a negative should be a learning experience, but one to avoid at all costs in the future.

Can you guess who are the greatest critics of dance ministry in the church? Yep. It's my colleagues. This is appropriate because they should have free reign to express concerns to me since we are a team together charged with shepherding and leading God's church. I love and respect these men and women and am aware that seminary trained, highly educated pastor types are more often not artistic types. I try to gently remind them of my purposes, and I acknowledge their concerns, often making changes or more carefully selecting pieces based on their input. Fortunately, following the choreography process outlined in this book makes this a minor issue.

Also, the worship pastor must have a strong sense of the purpose of dance ministry within the scope of worship and/or church ministries, and the ability to communicate that with clarity and gentleness. He or she must also have thick skin and courage to keep doing what's right and best for the body of Christ, which includes both head and heart dominant people. We are called to be both, people who love the Lord our God with all our hearts, minds, soul, and strength.

The Worship Pastor and His Congregation: Who Am I Leading? Where Are We Going?

The role of the worshiper is to glorify God. With that as the foundation of all worship ministry, the worship leader has an additional role, to indeed lead the people sitting before him to wholeheartedly worship God. The main question then is: What best helps my people enter into authentic worship of the Lord?

The best advice I heard early on as a worship leader is that my most important consideration is: Who am I leading? This helps you determine first of all what elements you include in the worship service.

How much teaching should you do? Make your philosophy of worship obvious and communicate it often.

How willing and eager to worship are your people? That will determine how much encouragement you should give to help them engage in worshiping the Lord.

What Scripture should you share that models authentic worship? What personal experiences should you share? How should you pray as the representative voice of the corporately gathered congregation? Where does the sermon fit in the flow of the worship service? Now consider whether a dance piece is appropriate, and what style would best minister to those you are leading.

Fortunately, we also consider another very important question: Where are we going, or who are we becoming? While we begin with who we are, we certainly must keep a forward thinking focus in mind. God is not interested in maintaining but in transforming. So we must always be focused on helping our congregation become better worshipers. Remember that our goal is the building up of the body of Christ: "until we all reach unity in the faith and in the knowledge of the Son of God and become mature, attaining to the whole measure of the fullness of Christ" (Ephesians 4:13). My gut tells me that mature worshipers attaining to the whole measure of the fullness of Christ will dance! With this in mind, a church that has not used or valued dance as a valid expression of praise within the worship service can and should be taught to do so. However, the vision of where we (the church) are going or who we are becoming must be a leadership supported and/or driven focus. Toward this end, the worship pastor must move together with the senior pastor, never pushing his own agenda.

Once you agree that dance should be part of the worship service, make sure that dance is a part of a bigger focus of valuing arts and artists in the church and giving them a voice in the worship service. Dance that accompanies praise and worship will almost always fit well and accomplish the core purpose of worship. After all, it is biblically encouraged. However, dance as a standalone special number in a church that rarely has musical solos (known as "special music" in my childhood church), dramas, films, or fine art will stand out like a sore thumb instead of one of the fingers on a healthy hand. It just won't feel like a good fit to most people. This creates awkwardness and confusion on the part of the congregants and becomes more of a distraction from worship rather than an encouragement toward worship. So my advice for churches that do not have a comprehensive arts ministry is to include dance only as a part of what's already happening. Picture it like another instrument in the band or voice in the congregation. This is at least the starting point from which a larger dance ministry that includes performance pieces could develop.

The Worship Pastor and His Choreographers

Artists are usually sensitive people. We take deep ownership and pride in our art. We put our hearts out there for the public to see and hear. Criticism is hard to take and is even harder to let go.

The worship leader or pastor must have a good relationship with his choreographers. We do need to evaluate our art because when we place it in the worship service, it must accomplish the purposes—to glorify God and build up the Body (the church). The worship leader must know and trust the heart of the choreographer and know that he or she is set on glorifying God 24/7. He must establish a basis to evaluate whether or not an artistic piece is accomplishing the purpose of building up the congregation. Their relationship must be based on trust and mutual respect. The worship pastor must not micromanage, yet have authority to respectfully make changes.

Both pastor and choreographer must acknowledge that interactions will get messy at times and establish the Colossians 3:12-14 principle as the foundation of their relationship. While the whole passage is a great guideline for all relationships, verse 12 outlines five foundational elements that ensure smooth operations: "Therefore, as God's chosen people, holy and dearly loved, clothe yourselves with compassion, kindness, humility, gentleness and patience." These five foundational elements coupled with good communication are the key to avoiding or at least minimizing messy situations. When you think about the importance of the costume in a dance piece, think about this costume as the most important for both the choreographer and worship leader to put on. Mary wears these clothes, and by God's grace, I strive to as well.

I am so grateful for the 10-year relationship we have, being partners together in worship ministries. Her confidence from knowing her position in Christ, as chosen, holy, and dearly loved, coupled with this five-piece costume truly makes her a beautiful person. I can say this too about the younger choreographers Mary has been mentoring. A commitment to wearing the 3:12 costume is what makes church ministry a joy even when it's a bit messy.

Conclusion

I confess that when I first was introduced to dance in the worship service, I didn't get it. Fortunately, the content of the song choices was so strong that the lyrics and music brought me to a place of worship. But, I closed my eyes for most of the dance. Eventually, a few dances down the road, I opened my eyes and with that my heart began to open too. The dancers' movement inspired worship. I was touched by the joy and delight on the dancers' faces and felt that delight growing in me. I found myself in tears one time and then elated with joy on another occasion. I was starting to get it. Then I became a participant on Easter Sunday, 2003. I'll never forget the experience standing on stage with eight other men singing while using my body to fully worship the Lord. The song was "In Christ Alone." Trained dancers surrounded strength with beauty. I was bowing, kneeling, raising hands, and lifting my eyes toward heaven, singing the lyrics with my body as well as my voice. I became a better worshiper through that experience—a fully integrated worshiper, with all my heart, mind, soul, and strength engaged.

So there you have it; dance ministry defined with four essentials that allow dancers and dance ministry to glorify God and communicate the gospel followed by the perspective of a worship pastor to help you to understand dance ministry from the lens of a non-dance leader. Of course, there is much more to learn, but the Lord Jesus will show all of us as we develop the skills and sensitivity to express visual faith in the ages to come. May God bless you as you engage with Jesus in Soul to Sole Choreography.

> *"Even as we witness unpolished dancing, here in our corporate gathering, we will be reminded that our goal as Christians is not to be polished and impressive, but to be true."*[71]

---

[71] W. David O. Taylor, "The Dangers: What Are the Dangers of Artmaking in the Church?" in *For the Beauty of the Church*, ed. W. David O. Taylor (Grand Rapids, MI: Baker Books, 2010), 159. Fair use.

Appendix A

Soul to Sole Covenant with Jesus

This is the Soul to Sole Covenant to know, listen to, and love Jesus. This is one way that God has grown my faith through the years. Be open to other ways that will help you to know, listen to, and love God and others. Enjoy.

I have included the definition of covenant below to help you understand what takes place when you enter into an agreement with God. This covenantal agreement is also the basis for the rehearsal and leadership covenant, which are explained in Chapters 2 and 5.

Covenant: A covenant is an agreement of a solemn and binding force. The concept of covenant between God and His people is one of the most important theological truths of the Bible. By making a covenant with Abraham, God promised to bless His descendants and to make them His special people. Abraham, in return, was to remain faithful to God and to serve as a channel through which God's blessings could flow to the rest of the world (Biblesoft, 2003).

The covenant you sign on the next sheet is an agreement between you and the Lord. No one but you will monitor your progress. There are five ways this covenant will help you discover the foundation for biblical values. Each item is explained below.

1. Learning about Jesus cultivates knowing God in a personal relationship. Buy an inexpensive copy of the New Testament and read it. Use a highlight pen and underline the word <u>love</u> (or another word you want to study) or synonyms for that word every time you see them. This exercise should be done daily from one minute to one hour or more. In other words, daily reading should have no specific time frame. In addition, memorize at least one Scripture verse every month during the duration of this covenant.

2. Listening to Jesus engages prayer with the Creator. During the dates of this agreement, pray daily. As you pray and as you deepen your walk

with God, ask God to reveal His will to you in your circumstances. "Help" is a great prayer. Don't forget to listen to God's voice after you pray.

3. Looking to Jesus involves looking for practical opportunities to intentionally put <u>love</u> into practice. Identify at least one opportunity a month.

4. Leaning on Jesus includes a structure of accountability. Accountability occurs weekly with a sister, a brother, or a group of committed Christ-followers. Scheduled meetings should include four areas of discussion: burden-bearing, encouragement, confession of sin, and any biblical discoveries about <u>love</u> (or another word you have studied) that participants want to share.

5. Living for Jesus emphasizes evangelism with an involvement in a mission or mission funding. A mission involvement can include a missions project at your church, but it can also include reaching out to neighbors in need and/or other circumstances. Ask God to help you see the needs of others and focus on being others-centered.

On a personal note: I tend to read Scripture and underline words and verses in an area that I struggle with. Is it hard for you to love others? Study love. Are you impatient with your kids? Study patience. Do you have trouble forgiving others? Study forgiveness. Are you sinning in a specific area? Study sin. Do you have a bad attitude? Study attitude. As I do this, God begins to change my heart, my mind, and my actions in the area I am reading about. Enjoy the process. The Lord Jesus is a wonderful Teacher.

My Soul to Sole Covenant with Jesus: (in this covenant example, I am using <u>love</u> but you can substitute any biblical word you want.).

I commit to growing deeper in my faith. I want to know more about <u>love</u>. As I grow in Christ, I want to discover how intentionally to engage in its cultivation. Therefore, at the end of the timeline for this covenant, I will celebrate practical "love stories" of how God has shown me how to "agape" and serve others through the application of Scripture and other spiritual building blocks. As God leads me, I will share these stories in personal and corporate church/ministry gatherings for the encouragement of the saints.

On a practical level, I will intentionally commit to daily Bible reading about <u>love</u> (that I will highlight) in the Old and/or New Testament. I will also memorize one Scripture verse every month that uses that word. Additionally, I will intentionally commit personal time to pray and to listen to God each day. Lastly, I will look for intentional opportunities to initiate <u>love</u> in my daily choices and I will intentionally meet for weekly fellowship and accountability with _____. Last, I will fund and/or involve myself in the following mission project(s):_____

Name _____

Starting date for Covenant _____

Completion date for Covenant _____

Appendix B

Book Resources on the Holy Spirit

If you find yourself overwhelmed with deciphering between "walking in the flesh" and "walking in the Spirit," check out these books that emphasize the importance of the Holy Spirit.

The Mystery of the Holy Spirit by R. C. Sproul

Forgotten God: Reversing our Tragic Neglect of the Holy Spirit by Francis Chan

Keep in Step with the Spirit: Finding Fullness in Our Walk with God by J. I. Packer

Surprised by the Power of the Spirit by Jack Deere

Hearing God: Developing a Conversational Relationship with God by Dallas Willard

Mystery of the Holy Spirit by A. W. Tozer

Here and Now: Living in the Spirit by Henri Nouwen

Fresh Wind, Fresh Fire: What Happens When God's Spirit Invades the Hearts of His People by Jim Cymbala

Authentic Christianity by Ray Stedman

Victory Over The Darkness by Neil Anderson.

Appendix C
Leadership Test

Excerpt taken from *Personality Plus* by Florence Littauer - used by permission

Introductory Explanation of Personalities

There's Only One You

Everyone wants a better personality. We all picture ourselves on Fantasy Island, where the ringing of the mission bells transforms us into articulate, attractively attired aristocrats. We no longer trip, fumble, spill, or grope; we converse, captivate, charm, and inspire. When the show is over, we switch off our mind-set and resume our test pattern of life. As we stare at our blank screens, we wonder why our "situation comedy" was canceled; why we've been replaced by the new stars who play their roles with confidence; why we seem to be cast as misfits.

We rush off to personality courses that promise to transform us into sparkling wits within twenty-four hours; self-evaluation experiences that will make us into minigods with maxipower; or sensitivity sessions, where we will feel our way into a fantastic future. We go expecting miracles and come home disappointed. We don't fit the mold of the exciting person, bursting with potential, pictured as the norm. We have different drives, abilities, and personalities—and we can't be treated as the same.

No Two Alike

If we were all identical eggs in a carton, a giant mother hen could warm us up and turn us into slick chicks or roving roosters overnight; but we are all different. We were all born with our own set of strengths and weaknesses, and no magic formula works wonders for all of us. Until we recognize our uniqueness, we can't understand how people can sit in the same seminar with the same speaker for the same amount of time and all achieve different degrees of success.

Personality Plus looks at each one of us as an individual blend of the four basic temperaments and encourages us to get acquainted with the *real me* underneath before trying to change what shows on the surface.

It's What's Underneath That Counts

When Michelangelo was ready to carve the statue of David, he spent a long time in selecting the marble, for he knew the quality of the raw material would determine the beauty of the finished product. He knew he could change the shape of the stone, but he couldn't transform the basic ingredient.

Every masterpiece he made was unique, for even if he had wanted to, he would not have been able to find a duplicate piece of marble. Even if he cut a block from the same quarry, it wouldn't have been exactly the same. Similar, yes, but not the same.

Each One of Us Is Unique

We started out with a combination of ingredients that made us different from our brothers and our sisters. Over the years people have chiseled on us, chipped, hammered, sanded, and buffed. Just when we thought we were finished products, someone would start shaping us up again. Occasionally we'd enjoy a day in the park, when everyone who passed by admired us and stroked us, but at other times we were ridiculed, analyzed, or ignored.

We were all born with our own temperament traits, our raw material, our own kind of rock. Some of us are granite, some marble, some alabaster, some sandstone. Our type of rock doesn't change, but our shapes can be altered. So it is with our personalities. We start with our own set of inborn traits. Some of our qualities are beautiful with strains of gold. Some are blemished with fault lines of gray. Our circumstances, IQ, nationality, economics, environment, and parental influence can mold our personalities, but the rock underneath remains the same.

My temperament is the real *me*; my personality is the dress I put on over me. I can look in the mirror in the morning and see a plain face, straight hair, and a bulgy body. That's the real me. Gratefully, within an hour I can apply makeup to create a colorful face; I can plug in the

PERSONALITY PROFILE

curling iron to fluff up my hair; and I can put on a flattering dress to camouflage too many curves. I've taken the real me and dressed it up, but I haven't permanently changed what's underneath.

If only we could understand ourselves:

Know *what* we're made of
Know *who* we really are
Know *why* we react as we do
Know our *strengths* and how to amplify them
Know our *weaknesses* and how to overcome them

We can! *Personality Plus* will show us how to examine ourselves, how to polish up our strengths, and how to chip away our weaknesses. When we know who we are and why we act the way we do, we can begin to understand our inner selves, improve our personalities, and learn to get along with others. We are not going to try to imitate someone else, put on a brighter dress or new tie, or cry over the kind of stone we're made from. We're going to do the very best we can with the raw material available.

In recent years manufacturers have found ways to duplicate some of the classic statues, and in any large gift store you may find dozens of Davids, walls of Washingtons, lines of Lincolns, replicas of Reagan, and clones of Cleopatra. Imitations abound, but there's only one *you*.

Where Do We Start?

How many of you have a Michelangelo complex? How many of you look at other people as raw material, ready to be carved up by your expert hand? How many of you can think of at least one person whom you could really shape up if only he'd listen to your words of wisdom? How anxious is he to hear from you?

If it were possible to remake other people, my husband, Fred, and I would be perfect, for we set out to chip away at each other right from the beginning. I knew that if he'd loosen up and have fun, we could have a good marriage; but *he* wanted me to straighten up and get organized. On our honeymoon I found out Fred and I didn't even agree on eating grapes!

. I always enjoyed plunking a whole bunch of cold, green grapes beside me and plucking off whichever one appealed to me. Until I married Fred, I didn't know there were "Grape Rules." I didn't know each simple pleasure in life had a so-called right way. Fred first brought up the Grape Rule as I was sitting on the patio outside our cottage at Cambridge Beaches in Bermuda, looking out to sea and absentmindedly pulling grapes off a large bunch. I didn't realize Fred was analyzing my unsystematic eating of the fruit until he asked, "Do you like grapes?"

"Oh, I love grapes!"

"Then I assume you'd like to know how to eat them correctly?"

On that I snapped out of my romantic reveries and asked a question that subsequently became a part of a regular routine: "What did I do wrong?"

"It's not that you're doing it *wrong*; you're just *not* doing it right." I couldn't see that there was much of a difference, but I phrased it his way.

"What am I not doing right?"

"Anyone knows that to eat grapes properly, you cut off a little bunch at a time, like this."

Fred pulled out his nail clippers and snipped off a small cluster of grapes, which he set before me.

As he stood smugly staring down at me, I asked, "Does this make them taste better?"

"It's not for taste. It's so the large bunch will keep its looks longer. The way *you* eat them—just grabbing grapes here and there—leaves the bunch a wreck. Look at what you've done to it! See all those tiny bare stems, sticking up all over the place? They ruin the shape of the whole bunch." I glanced around the secluded patio to see if there was some hidden group of grape judges waiting to enter my bunch in a contest, but seeing none, I said, "Who cares?"

I had not yet learned that "Who cares?" was not a statement to make to Fred, because it caused him to turn red and sigh with hopelessness, "*I* care, and that should be enough."

PERSONALITY PROFILE

Fred did really care about every detail in life, and my presence in his family did seem to ruin the shape of the whole bunch. To help me out, Fred diligently set out to improve me. Instead of appreciating his wisdom, I tried to sabotage his strategy and subtly change him to become more like me. For years Fred chiseled and chipped away at my failures—and I sanded steadily on his fault lines—but neither one of us improved.

It was not until we first read *Spirit Controlled Temperament* (Tyndale House) by Tim LaHaye that our eyes were opened to what we were doing. Each of us was trying to remake the other. We didn't realize someone could be different and still not be wrong. I found I am a Popular Sanguine who loves fun and excitement; Fred is a Perfect Melancholy who wants life to be serious and orderly.

As we began to read and study the temperaments further, we discovered we were both also somewhat Powerful Choleric, the type who is always right and knows *everything*. No wonder we didn't get along! Not only were we opposites in our personalities and interests in life, but each one of us knew we were the only one who was right. Can you picture such a marriage?

What a relief it was to find there *was* hope for us; we *could* understand each other's temperaments and accept each other's personalities. As our lives changed, we began to teach, research, and write on the temperaments. *Personality Plus* is the culmination of twenty-five years of seminar speaking, personality counseling, and day-by-day observation of people's temperaments. This book will provide a quick psychology lesson in easy, enjoyable terms so that we may:

1. Examine our own strengths and weaknesses and learn how to accentuate our positives and eliminate our negatives.
2. Understand other people and realize that just because others are different does not make them wrong.

To find our own raw material and understand our basic natures, we will examine the personality or temperament groupings first established by Hippocrates twenty-four hundred years ago. We will have fun with the Popular Sanguines, who exude enthusiasm. We'll get serious with the Perfect Melancholies, who strive for perfection in all things. We'll charge forth with the Powerful Cholerics, who are born leaders. And we'll relax with the Peaceful Phlegmatics, who are happily reconciled to life. No matter who we are, we have something to learn from each of these types.

Your Personality Profile

Before we are introduced to the four different types of temperaments, take a few minutes to check off your own Personality Profile, which was compiled by Fred. When you have completed the forty questions according to the directions, transfer your marks to the score sheet and add up your totals. If you are a Popular Sanguine and get confused by columns, find a serious Perfect Melancholy who sees life as a series of statistics and ask for help in adding up your assets and your liabilities.

No one is 100 percent of any temperament, but your score will give you an accurate view of your basic strengths and weaknesses. If you come up with even scores all around, you are probably Peaceful Phlegmatic, the all-purpose person.

Your Personality Profile is unlike any others, but the general information in your temperament pattern will be valuable in understanding yourself and in learning to accept others as they are. As you encourage your family and friends to analyze themselves, you will open up new avenues of communication that will be both enlightening and entertaining.

When you have scored your temperament test, you will have some idea of your inner traits—your inborn characteristics that cause you to respond to circumstances as you do. To get a deeper understanding of the *real* you, follow the next five chapters and learn something new about yourself.

When he, the Spirit of truth, is come, he will guide you into all truth.

John 16:13

Your Personality Profile

Directions—In each of the following rows of *four words across*, place an X in front of the *one* word that most often applies to you. Continue through all forty lines; be sure each number is marked. If you are not sure which word "most applies," ask a spouse or a friend, and think of what your answer would have been *when you were a child*. (Full definitions for each of these words begin on page 195.)

Strengths

1 ___ Adventurous	___ Adaptable	___ Animated	___ Analytical
2 ___ Persistent	___ Playful	___ Persuasive	___ Peaceful
3 ___ Submissive	___ Self-sacrificing	___ Sociable	___ Strong-willed
4 ___ Considerate	___ Controlled	___ Competitive	___ Convincing
5 ___ Refreshing	___ Respectful	___ Reserved	___ Resourceful
6 ___ Satisfied	___ Sensitive	___ Self-reliant	___ Spirited
7 ___ Planner	___ Patient	___ Positive	___ Promoter
8 ___ Sure	___ Spontaneous	___ Scheduled	___ Shy
9 ___ Orderly	___ Obliging	___ Outspoken	___ Optimistic
10 ___ Friendly	___ Faithful	___ Funny	___ Forceful
11 ___ Daring	___ Delightful	___ Diplomatic	___ Detailed
12 ___ Cheerful	___ Consistent	___ Cultured	___ Confident
13 ___ Idealistic	___ Independent	___ Inoffensive	___ Inspiring
14 ___ Demonstrative	___ Decisive	___ Dry humor	___ Deep
15 ___ Mediator	___ Musical	___ Mover	___ Mixes easily
16 ___ Thoughtful	___ Tenacious	___ Talker	___ Tolerant
17 ___ Listener	___ Loyal	___ Leader	___ Lively
18 ___ Contented	___ Chief	___ Chartmaker	___ Cute
19 ___ Perfectionist	___ Pleasant	___ Productive	___ Popular
20 ___ Bouncy	___ Bold	___ Behaved	___ Balanced

PERSONALITY PROFILE

Weaknesses

21 ___ Blank	___ Bashful	___ Brassy	___ Bossy
22 ___ Undisciplined	___ Unsympathetic	___ Unenthusiastic	___ Unforgiving
23 ___ Reticent	___ Resentful	___ Resistant	___ Repetitious
24 ___ Fussy	___ Fearful	___ Forgetful	___ Frank
25 ___ Impatient	___ Insecure	___ Indecisive	___ Interrupts
26 ___ Unpopular	___ Uninvolved	___ Unpredictable	___ Unaffectionate
27 ___ Headstrong	___ Haphazard	___ Hard to please	___ Hesitant
28 ___ Plain	___ Pessimistic	___ Proud	___ Permissive
29 ___ Angered easily	___ Aimless	___ Argumentative	___ Alienated
30 ___ Naive	___ Negative attitude	___ Nervy	___ Nonchalant
31 ___ Worrier	___ Withdrawn	___ Workaholic	___ Wants credit
32 ___ Too sensitive	___ Tactless	___ Timid	___ Talkative
33 ___ Doubtful	___ Disorganized	___ Domineering	___ Depressed
34 ___ Inconsistent	___ Introvert	___ Intolerant	___ Indifferent
35 ___ Messy	___ Moody	___ Mumbles	___ Manipulative
36 ___ Slow	___ Stubborn	___ Show-off	___ Skeptical
37 ___ Loner	___ Lord over others	___ Lazy	___ Loud
38 ___ Sluggish	___ Suspicious	___ Short-tempered	___ Scatterbrained
39 ___ Revengeful	___ Restless	___ Reluctant	___ Rash
40 ___ Compromising	___ Critical	___ Crafty	___ Changeable

Personality Scoring Sheet

Now transfer all your X's to the corresponding words on the Personality Scoring Sheet and add up your totals. For example, if you checked Animated on the profile, check it on the scoring sheet. (Note: The words are in a different order on the profile and the scoring sheet.)

Strengths

Popular Sanguine	Powerful Choleric	Perfect Melancholy	Peaceful Phlegmatic
1 ___ Animated	___ Adventurous	___ Analytical	___ Adaptable
2 ___ Playful	___ Persuasive	___ Persistent	___ Peaceful
3 ___ Sociable	___ Strong-willed	___ Self-sacrificing	___ Submissive
4 ___ Convincing	___ Competitive	___ Considerate	___ Controlled
5 ___ Refreshing	___ Resourceful	___ Respectful	___ Reserved
6 ___ Spirited	___ Self-reliant	___ Sensitive	___ Satisfied
7 ___ Promoter	___ Positive	___ Planner	___ Patient
8 ___ Spontaneous	___ Sure	___ Scheduled	___ Shy
9 ___ Optimistic	___ Outspoken	___ Orderly	___ Obliging
10 ___ Funny	___ Forceful	___ Faithful	___ Friendly
11 ___ Delightful	___ Daring	___ Detailed	___ Diplomatic
12 ___ Cheerful	___ Confident	___ Cultured	___ Consistent
13 ___ Inspiring	___ Independent	___ Idealistic	___ Inoffensive
14 ___ Demonstrative	___ Decisive	___ Deep	___ Dry humor
15 ___ Mixes easily	___ Mover	___ Musical	___ Mediator
16 ___ Talker	___ Tenacious	___ Thoughtful	___ Tolerant
17 ___ Lively	___ Leader	___ Loyal	___ Listener
18 ___ Cute	___ Chief	___ Chartmaker	___ Contented
19 ___ Popular	___ Productive	___ Perfectionist	___ Pleasant
20 ___ Bouncy	___ Bold	___ Behaved	___ Balanced

Totals—Strengths

_____   _____   _____   _____

PERSONALITY PROFILE

Weaknesses

	Popular Sanguine	Powerful Choleric	Perfect Melancholy	Peaceful Phlegmatic
21	Brassy	Bossy	Bashful	Blank
22	Undisciplined	Unsympathetic	Unforgiving	Unenthusiastic
23	Repetitious	Resistant	Resentful	Reticent
24	Forgetful	Frank	Fussy	Fearful
25	Interrupts	Impatient	Insecure	Indecisive
26	Unpredictable	Unaffectionate	Unpopular	Uninvolved
27	Haphazard	Headstrong	Hard to please	Hesitant
28	Permissive	Proud	Pessimistic	Plain
29	Angered easily	Argumentative	Alienated	Aimless
30	Naive	Nervy	Negative attitude	Nonchalant
31	Wants credit	Workaholic	Withdrawn	Worrier
32	Talkative	Tactless	Too sensitive	Timid
33	Disorganized	Domineering	Depressed	Doubtful
34	Inconsistent	Intolerant	Introvert	Indifferent
35	Messy	Manipulative	Moody	Mumbles
36	Show-off	Stubborn	Skeptical	Slow
37	Loud	Lord over others	Loner	Lazy
38	Scatterbrained	Short-tempered	Suspicious	Sluggish
39	Restless	Rash	Revengeful	Reluctant
40	Changeable	Crafty	Critical	Compromising

Totals—Weaknesses

____ ____ ____ ____

Combined Totals

____ ____ ____ ____

This test is very easy to interpret. Once you've transferred your answers to the scoring sheet, added up your total number of answers in each of the four columns, and added your totals from both the strengths and weaknesses sections, you'll know your dominant personality type. You'll also know what combination you are. If, for example, your score is 15 in Powerful Choleric strengths and weaknesses, there's really little question. You're almost all Powerful Choleric. But if your score is, for example, 8 in Popular Sanguine, 6 in Perfect Melancholy, and 2 in each of the others, you're a Popular Sanguine with a strong Perfect Melancholy. You'll also, of course, know your least dominant type.

As you read the following pages and work with the material in this book, you'll learn how to put your strengths to work for you, how to compensate for the weaknesses in your dominant type, and how to understand the strengths and weaknesses of other types.

A Brief Explanation of Personalities

PERSONALITY POTENTIAL

You've taken the test. Now you know what personality or combination you are. Following are the strengths of each summarized. Bet you didn't know you had all this going for you! Now that you know your particular assets—make them work for you.

Popular Sanguine Personality

The Extrovert • The Talker • The Optimist

STRENGTHS

POPULAR SANGUINE'S EMOTIONS

Appealing personality
Talkative, storyteller
Life of the party
Good sense of humor
Memory for color
Physically holds on to listener
Emotional and demonstrative
Enthusiastic and expressive
Cheerful and bubbling over
Curious
Good on stage
Wide-eyed and innocent
Lives in the present
Changeable disposition
Sincere at heart
Always a child

POPULAR SANGUINE AS A PARENT

Makes home fun
Is liked by children's friends
Turns disaster into humor
Is the circus master

POPULAR SANGUINE AT WORK

Volunteers for jobs
Thinks up new activities
Looks great on the surface
Creative and colorful
Has energy and enthusiasm
Starts in a flashy way
Inspires others to join
Charms others to work

POPULAR SANGUINE AS A FRIEND

Makes friends easily
Loves people
Thrives on compliments
Seems exciting
Envied by others
Doesn't hold grudges
Apologizes quickly
Prevents dull moments
Likes spontaneous activities

Perfect Melancholy Personality

The Introvert • The Thinker • The Pessimist

STRENGTHS

PERFECT MELANCHOLY'S EMOTIONS

Deep and thoughtful
Analytical
Serious and purposeful
Genius prone
Talented and creative
Artistic or musical
Philosophical and poetic
Appreciative of beauty
Sensitive to others
Self-sacrificing
Conscientious
Idealistic

PERFECT MELANCHOLY AS A PARENT

Sets high standards
Wants everything done right
Keeps home in good order
Picks up after children
Sacrifices own will for others
Encourages scholarship and
    talent

PERFECT MELANCHOLY AT WORK

Schedule oriented
Perfectionist, high standards
Detail conscious
Persistent and thorough
Orderly and organized
Neat and tidy
Economical
Sees the problems
Finds creative solutions
Needs to finish what is started
Likes charts, graphs, figures,
    lists

PERFECT MELANCHOLY AS A FRIEND

Makes friends cautiously
Content to stay in background
Avoids causing attention
Faithful and devoted
Will listen to complaints
Can solve others' problems
Deep concern for other people
Moved to tears with compassion
Seeks ideal mate

PERSONALITY POTENTIAL

Powerful Choleric Personality

The Extrovert • The Doer • The Optimist

STRENGTHS

POWERFUL CHOLERIC'S EMOTIONS

Born leader
Dynamic and active
Compulsive need for change
Must correct wrongs
Strong willed and decisive
Unemotional
Not easily discouraged
Independent and self-sufficient
Exudes confidence
Can run anything

POWERFUL CHOLERIC AS A PARENT

Exerts sound leadership
Establishes goals
Motivates family to action
Knows the right answer
Organizes household

POWERFUL CHOLERIC AT WORK

Goal oriented
Sees the whole picture
Organizes well
Seeks practical solutions
Moves quickly to action
Delegates work
Insists on production
Makes the goal
Stimulates activity
Thrives on opposition

POWERFUL CHOLERIC AS A FRIEND

Has little need for friends
Will work for group activity
Will lead and organize
Is usually right
Excels in emergencies

A Look at Our Individual Assets

Peaceful Phlegmatic Personality

The Introvert • The Watcher • The Pessimist

STRENGTHS

PEACEFUL PHLEGMATIC'S EMOTIONS

Low-key personality
Easygoing and relaxed
Calm, cool, and collected
Patient, well balanced
Consistent life
Quiet but witty
Sympathetic and kind
Keeps emotions hidden
Happily reconciled to life
All-purpose person

PEACEFUL PHLEGMATIC AS A PARENT

Makes a good parent
Takes time for the children
Is not in a hurry
Can take the good with the bad
Doesn't get upset easily

PEACEFUL PHLEGMATIC AT WORK

Competent and steady
Peaceful and agreeable
Has administrative ability
Mediates problems
Avoids conflicts
Good under pressure
Finds the easy way

PEACEFUL PHLEGMATIC AS A FRIEND

Easy to get along with
Pleasant and enjoyable
Inoffensive
Good listener
Dry sense of humor
Enjoys watching people
Has many friends
Has compassion and concern

For further information on the personalities at work read *Personality Puzzle*, by Florence and Marita Littauer (Revell, 1992).

Appendix D

Leadership/Choreography Covenant

I wish to participate at ____Church/Ministry using my gifts as a leader and/or choreographer, honoring the Lord Jesus through prayer-in-motion. With grace as the foundation, I agree to the following:

a. All of the conditions listed in the dance ministry member covenant used for the preparation of any prayer-in-motion. (See Chapter 5.)

b. I want to grow in my personal relationship with Jesus. Because of that, I will spend daily time knowing God, listening to God, and loving God and others. List the personal Bible study you are involved in:_____.

c. I commit to be transparent if any disagreements should occur within the context of movement preparation and I commit to speak directly to the person(s) involved. I will use electronic or personal communication with the ministry supervisor regarding any incidents. A decision not to gossip with others will be the philosophical foundation of all interaction.

d. d. I commit to display an attitude of submission to the leaders above me—whether in agreement with those decisions or not—as well as openness to preview input in reference to choreography, music, and costuming choices.

e. I commit to the study of the biblical concept being choreographed.

f. I resolve to have the integrity to complete any individual project responsibilities agreed upon and to follow through with administrative communication (using a cc format in emails) and completion of the dance/rehearsal process. Active membership at _____ Church.

g. I commit to my attendance as leader/choreographer (and attendance of individual choreographers if a program rotates choreographers) at pastoral planning meetings.

h. I commit to consistent meetings (as requested) with ____ regarding growth in faith and Bible study, personal interactions with dancers, and the choreography process.

Date: _____

Signature of leader/choreographer: _____

Name of motion prayer: _____

Biblical concept targeted for choreography: _____

Appendix E

Book Resources on Choreography

All the books below will provide enrichment as you develop skill in choreography creation. The first book has a philosophical base for choreography, and the second one is a practical resource to understand how to implement movement in choreography creation. It is outstanding. The rest will supplement your understanding of movement creation. Use as you feel led.

1. * Doris Humphrey's The Art of Making Dances (considered a classic in the field of choreography).

2. * Anne Green Gilbert's Creative Dance for All Ages: A Conceptual Approach (systematically develops a focused way to understand the choreography tools of time, space, force, and body).

3. Jan Erkert's Harnessing the Wind: the Art of Teaching Modern Dance.

4. Lynne Anne Blom's The Intimate Act of Choreography.

5. Twyla Tharp's The Creative Habit: Learn it and Use It for Life.

*most important resource

Appendix F

Technical and Genesis Phrase Creation

Name of song and/or project: _____

Circle category of worship: praise, beauty (healing), teaching, celebration, and/or prayer.

Identified biblical concept: _____

Circle what type of phrase you will create below:

TECHNICAL PHRASE CREATION

1. Design a technical movement phrase and label technical phrases with numbers for easy identification, i.e. "Technical Phrase #1" and so forth.

2. Include the counts for this phrase.

3. Type out the movement phrases with technical dance terms.

GENESIS PHRASE CREATION (use movement Tools 3-5 from Chapter 3)

1. Look at the list of descriptive movement words below [a-c]:

   a. Locomotor movement, non-locomotor movement

   b. Movement qualities: percussive, sustained, pendular, collapse, suspend, vibratory, silence

   c. Dance elements:

Time: speed-slow, medium, fast; rhythm-pulse, breath, pattern, accent;

Space: place-self & general; level-low, medium, high; size-big, medium, little, near-reach, far-reach; direction- forward, backward, right side, left side, up, down; pathway-straight, curved, zig-zag; focus-single focus, multi focus;

Force: energy-smooth, sharp; weight-strong, light; flow-free, bound;

Body: body parts, body shapes-symmetrical, asymmetrical, curved straight, angular, twisted, relationship, balance

2. Begin to create a written genesis phrase in the blank space below or on the back of this sheet.

   Write a genesis movement description for every one to two lines of song lyrics. Begin each section of the written genesis movement phrase by specifying:

   a. either locomotor or non-locomotor movement

   b. a specific quality of movement (if you have one)

   c. add in other descriptive movement words to complete the phrase as you are led by the Spirit

3. Movement descriptions are not limited to movement tools 3-5 in Chapter 3. Feel free to add any movement descriptions that you wish.

4. When you are ready to prepare a dance, type out the genesis phrase descriptions and give them to the dancers during one of the early rehearsals (labeling them "Genesis Phrase #1," etc.). Ask them to create movements to go with each genesis phrase description. Initially, don't share song lyrics based on the genesis description with dancers.

5. Video/phone record the created movement developed during the genesis part of rehearsal.

Appendix G

The Rehearsal Covenant

I wish to participate at _____ Church honoring the Lord Jesus through prayer-in-motion.

I agree to the following:

1. Mandatory rehearsal as designated by dance ministry participants.

2. The desire to share the Gospel through the visual arts.

3. A heart that would encourage rather than discourage as well as the commitment to speak the truth in love when it is necessary.

4. Confidentiality of personal prayer requests shared.

5. A commitment to pray for those participating in this dance as well as for those who watch.

6. An encouragement to study the Bible daily so as to be sensitive to God's personal life direction as well as His leading in the design of the motion prayer being rehearsed.

7. A pledge of moral purity as taught in Scripture.

8. An commitment to check out a CD or listen to the song on an IPOD or Internet connection with a encouragement to practice the worship dance being rehearsed at least one time per day until it is shared.

9. Release: I authorize unlimited use of my photograph/video along with any ministry dances in which I have participated. I waive any claim for compensation. I also waive any right to inspect the finished work or approve the use to which it may be applied. I certify that I fully understand the meaning of this release and

because I intend for it to be legally binding, I am signing this sheet.

Date:_____

Name of Dance:_____

Names of Participants:

1.

2.

3.

4.

Appendix H

Evaluation Form for Dance Preview

Name of previewer:_____

Name of dance:_____

Date: _____

Write out the biblical concept that the movement and words in the song or text communicate: _____

Evaluate: (1 to 10)	Rate (1 to 10)	Comments
Overall response to dance		
Communication of biblical concept		
Technical level clean and clear		
Costumes		
Music		
Unaddressed problems?		
Worship level of dancers		

Appendix I

Timeline for Dance Choreographers:

1. Meet to choose a ministry song to choreograph with the approval of worship pastor. Be prepared to submit some ideas if you are asked. When song is chosen, talk to worship pastor about a dance statement for congregation.

2. Download lyrics of song online or ask church office to email words to your email for inductive analysis. Order individual DVDs for each dancer.

3. Meet with dance leader and sign leadership covenant.

4. Email/call with church staff to see what the decorations will be for the ministry date you have; make sure that costumes and props coordinate with other colors onstage.

5. Find out the church budget you have and, if necessary, order props/costumes as soon as possible. (Sometimes companies cannot supply articles in time.)

6. Study identified biblical concept that you are choreographing during the process of the dance.

7. Two-to-three weeks before the start of rehearsals, identify the potential date that will start rehearsals. Call/email the church office and reserve the rehearsal room for that date.

8. Send out an email to dancers inviting them to participate. Give yourself two weeks to choreograph before the start of rehearsals so that you can plan choreography without stress. Give yourself six weeks of rehearsal time (allows for 6-8 rehearsals). Make sure that you request dancers to respond to you as quickly as possible so that you can plan choreography easier.

9. Print out these the song lyrics and a dance score for the first rehearsal. Sign the rehearsal covenant with dancers. You can include brief research on the biblical concept you have identified to share with dancers during the first rehearsal.

10. Meet for the first rehearsal and schedule the rest of the rehearsals for the dance, telling the group that these rehearsals must have office approval before they are final. Go home from this rehearsal and email church staff with all the proposed times, dates, and room reservations. When she emails you back (hopefully with approval), email all dancers with final rehearsal schedule.

   IF THIS IS A CHRISTMAS OR EASTER SERVICE, FIND OUT WHEN THE FINAL/DRESS TECH IS FROM THE WORSHIP PASTOR.

11. Let dancers know if rehearsal schedule is approved. Email dancers once a week with dance encouragement and details of dance rehearsals.

12. Finalize costume and prop choices by the third rehearsal. During weekly email, let dancers know when they can size costumes. Feel free to do this 15 minutes before or after rehearsals if you need full rehearsal time.

13. Four-to-five weeks before ministry presentation, email media and sound with information about the dance, if you need them to collaborate with you in any way.

14. Four-to-five weeks before ministry presentation, always email lighting crew with song lyrics and dance presentation; invite them to see the dance one time before the final dress/tech. Send them the rehearsal schedule for the dance. Ask them to be there for the final dress/tech so that lighting is finalized prior to presentation. If you have multiple lighting cues for them, note these on the lyric sheet that you send them via email.

15. Four-to-five weeks prior to presentation, prepare a statement about the dance process for the congregation for display. Send in all

information as soon as possible as sometimes it takes a while for the administrative staff to do all the things that they do to make this happen in a timely fashion.

16.   Four-to-five weeks before presentation, email elders, pastoral staff, and/or mature Christ followers to review dance. Give them at least two times that they can come and preview dance. Ask them to confirm their attendance. Print out forms and have them ready.

17.   Make sure you have the email addresses of the following

Worship pastor:
Worship assistant:
Lighting:
Sound:
Media:
Video:
Stage manager:

Appendix J

A Deeper Look at Costume Choice

The Big Picture

How does this costume choice relate to God's truth? Is it biblical?

When it comes to the subject of modest clothing, the first question we should ask ourselves is: What am I trying to accomplish by what I wear? In the case of dance ministry, it is to reflect worship and to lead the congregation in visual worship of Jesus. It should never distract those who watch.

- Do the costumes and movement choices distract the congregation or reflect God's standards of holiness?

- Is there a bigger picture that this issue relates to?

Pornography is a public health issue in a sexualized culture. Movements and clothing can lead congregants away from worship in spirit and truth. We are de-sensitized to modest clothing and movement in this culture.

One pastor courageously requested, "Please, no tight clothing and/or open crotch movement." For men and women struggling with pornography, tightness on any clothing area equals seeing skin. Look for current articles and statistics by checking the National Center on Sexual Exploitation (NCOSE) (endsexualexploitation.org).

Because dance relies on the body to communicate its language and because the body is the vehicle for worship as the temple of the Holy Spirit, we must carefully consider what we wear and go the extra mile when it comes to God honoring clothing and movement choices.

Consider what these Bible verses teach on this issue:

"Do you not know that your bodies are temples of the Holy Spirit?" (1Corinthians 6:19).

"I urge you, brothers and sisters, in view of God's mercy, to offer your bodies as a living sacrifice, holy and pleasing to God—this is true and proper worship" (Romans 12:1).

"I also want women to dress modestly, with decency and propriety, not with braided hair or gold or pearls or expensive clothes, but with good deeds, appropriate for women who profess to worship God" (1 Timothy 2:9-10).

"It is better not to eat meat or drink wine or to do anything else that will cause your brother to fall" (Romans 14:21).

(See garment guidelines outlined in Chapters 5 and 6 of this book.)

Summary of Costume Criteria: no distraction from the worship of Jesus.

- Modest:

    Dresses that fall below the knee (i.e. a beautiful sack with a belt).

    Pants should never be stretched tight on hips, thighs, rear, or crotch area.

    Blouses should never be pressed tight on the bust area.

- Artistic to the concept and style of music (often beauty).
- Washable.
- Simple (not distracting from worship).

Today's Culture

Secular clothing does not usually reflect God's requirements unless there is careful selection. Current dance attire does not often reflect God's requirements for worship; remember that dance becomes worship when presented at a church; because of that, the criteria is completely different. Any time your dance ministry acquires a new outfit, it requires a lot of planning, godly intentionality, and prayer.

The goal with thoughtful costume considerations is:

- To honor and give glory to God through the worship of Jesus.

- Protection of dance ministry as a communication and worship vehicle in the church.

- Protection of worship pastor.

- Protection of choreographer.

- Protection of men and women who struggle with sexual issues.

- Protection of women not to be objectified.

It is through submission to God's ways of doing things that we can be at peace when we choose costumes in a culture that is increasingly immodest.

Research

"Immodesty can be put in perspective when women understand the stronghold that lust and pornography have on men today. The pornography industry in the United States rakes in 12 billion dollars a year. Surveys taken by Promise Keepers, Focus on the Family, Insight for Living, and other reputable Christian organizations show about half of the male respondents indicated they've viewed porn within the past few months. Did you get that? If this statistic is correct, five of 10 men you see in church have looked at porn recently. Some of them have looked at it daily. And who knows how many more of the 'innocent' 50 percent have recently leafed through a bikini magazine or watched steamy R-rated movies?"

"Tips on dressing modestly: Styles come and go, but class is always in fashion. Keep skirts at knee level, and don't wear tight shirts or jeans. Exposed belly buttons, backs, underwear, and mid riffs aren't appropriate in mixed company. Choose pants that don't have writing on the seat, or else you're asking men to stare at your butt."[73]

What sort of atmosphere do you create in your home or church? Women need to ask if they are causing their brothers to stumble by their choices of dress. One man says, "If you only knew how much your outfit caused me to stumble, you wouldn't dress that way."

---

[73] Kevin L. Howard "One Man's Plea for Christian Women to Dress Modestly." NeedNotFret.com..

God holds men and women to a higher standard. It's easy to be immersed in the culture and be unaware of dress choices.

According to a study by Covenant Eyes, roughly 39 percent of all professing Christian men and 13 percent of all professing Christian women believe that their use of pornography is excessive. Other reports indicate the problem could be even more extensive. Whatever the exact numbers, porn is a major problem, and that's connected to its accessibility.[74]

In another research study by Proven Men Ministries, with the Barna Group, two-thirds of all Christian men have visited Internet pornography sites and struggle with them. More and more women are also accessing Internet pornography.[75]

Let's clarify the costume decisions that we make in dance ministry so that we honor the Lord Jesus in modest dress as we worship Him in spirit and in truth.

---

[74] 2014 Covenant Eyes, "Pornography Statistics" http://www.covenanteyes.com/resources/download-your-copy-of-the-pornography-statistics-pack/.

[75] Proven Men Ministries, conducted by the Barna Group, 2014 Pornography Survey and Statistics (http://www.ProvenMen.org/2014pornsurvey

Mary M. Bawden is available for speaking engagements and public appearances. For more information contact:

Mary M. Bawden
C/O Advantage Books
P.O. Box 160847
Altamonte Springs, FL 32716

info@ advbooks.com

To purchase additional copies of this book or other books published by Advantage Books call our order number at:

407-788-3110 (Book Orders Only)

or visit our bookstore website at:
www.advbookstore.com

Also available as an eBook: ISBN 9781597553919

Longwood, Florida, USA
"we bring dreams to life"™
www.advbookstore.com

CPSIA information can be obtained
at www.ICGtesting.com
Printed in the USA
FSHW021959220519
58383FS

9 781597 553834